Heirs together

Heirs together

establishing intergenerational Cell Church

Daphne Kirk

Kevin
Mayhew

This edition published in 1998 by
KEVIN MAYHEW LTD
Buxhall
Stowmarket
Suffolk IP14 3DJ

0 1 2 3 4 5 6 7 8 9

ISBN 1 84003 276 6
Catalogue No 1500236

Cover design by Jaquetta Sergeant
Edited by Helen Elliot
Typesetting by Louise Selfe
Printed and bound in Great Britain

Contents

*This book is dedicated to my pastors,
Tony and Margaret Cornell,
and all the members of Ely Christian Fellowship
who are reaching out across the generations.*

*My thanks must go to my children,
in particular Andrew and Daniella,
who have patiently supported me during my
many hours spent putting this book together
and prayed for me as I have taken this message
to people from so many different nations.
Without their support and co-operation none
of this would have been possible.*

Foreword

A personal testimony from Tony and Margaret Cornell, Pastors of Ely Christian Fellowship, an Intergenerational Cell Church.

Pastors must carry the vision and be convinced in their own hearts that inter-generational values are the way forward for their Church. The following testimony will probably reflect struggles that most pastors confront as they move into this vision. However, with prayer and perseverance, there is much fruit!

For thirteen years we were a highly organised Church, with many good programmes. When we knew that God was telling us to make the transition into Cell Church, the question arose about the place of children in the cell. My first reaction was that the cell meeting would not be suitable for them and that adults would not want them there anyway. Many times I had heard it said that parents were glad to have a night out without their children, or that the children needed to be in bed early. However, for most families this would mean that only one parent at a time could attend the cell meeting while the other babysat.

Then we began to hear things that challenged us to think again. In America we saw children and youth in cells, so on returning to England we began to look into Scripture to see what the Word of God said about the place of children in the body of Christ. We were convicted that it was not God's way to exclude our children.

We therefore started to preach about what we found and to suggest that people could take their children to the cell meeting. As the Holy Spirit spoke clearly to the Church, we changed from saying that people could take children if they wanted, to actively encouraging them to do so. This was not an easy task, although many embraced the idea quickly.

I don't know why, but we had always considered that children and youth either wouldn't want to, or couldn't, join in with what we were doing in church. Their behaviour in services certainly seemed to indicate that, so we removed them and provided separate peer groups for them with their own curriculum. However, we were distressed to find that many teenagers fell away from the church and considered it boring. They never made the jump from their peer groups to the adult congregation. We thought that we had done the very best we could for our children and blamed Satan! Little did we dream that we were helping him do his evil work by our own church system which gave children and youth what they *seemed* to want. We did not realise that we were thinking like the world, rather than like God. Our system was giving children and youth the message that they couldn't join in with us, that they weren't wanted and they would be bored. No wonder they could not wait to get out! Wouldn't you want to leave somewhere where you felt you weren't wanted? We discovered that 'something boring' is something that you just don't feel part of, and this goes for adults too!

The more we examined Scripture, the more we saw children ministering to the Lord, hearing God, seeing miracles, rejoicing alongside everyone else. In both the Old and New Testament we see God's concern for the generations. We therefore included our children in the cells, expecting them to be fully participating members. We gave the over-13s the opportunity of being members of a different intergenerational cell if they wanted to be separate from their parents. Slowly our people swung from nervous acceptance to warmly embracing these ideas as they saw with amazement the effect this had on the youth, children and adults.

Our next step was to think about having intergenerational celebrations. We had all had enough of the old-style family services and were determined that this would be a step forward into something new rather than a step back! We began simply by taking a look at what we were doing through the eyes of the youngsters, and making adjustments to our Sunday timetable, thinking carefully about how we presented the Word, how we worshipped, and so on. We also took steps to enable them to participate.

However, it was essential to pray, preach, teach and talk about the vision. None of this would have been possible without strategy and prayer. Many times we wanted to give up because it seemed an uphill task, it seemed too difficult. We forgot that children need time to change, just like adults. After all, it was a complete paradigm shift for them too!

We ended up with something that was far better for everyone!

We are now seeing children take their place as ministers in the body, because they are participating in the ministering unit of the body – their cell. They minister with adults and youth, they minister to adults and youth. We see them taking a full part in the worship service as well as prayer meetings and weeks of prayer. They are in the worship team, they usher, they serve communion, they pray for people. It used to be that they watched whilst most of the adults responded. Now they respond – they know that whatever is said from the front of the church is for them too!

Church has become their church too!

Introduction

The vision which has inspired me for over thirty years, and which I have actively sought to pass on to others, is of a church which includes all ages (children, young people and adults) in every aspect of its life. This is the vision of the intergenerational Church. In other words, I have read in the Word of God that He intends us to flow together and for *each generation to be a source of blessing to the other*, and so have expected to see this in our churches. To some extent this has happened, but never totally and consistently.

It seemed many churches knew that the children should be an integral part of the body but they did not know how to bring this about. It also seemed that people were deeply entrenched in the belief that young people would never want to be part of a church where they took their place among the adults and children.

For myself, and others who had the same vision, it felt like being a lone voice in the desert. There did not seem to be a truly effective way of walking out what I believed the Word of God said. I knew in my heart that *if God said it was possible, it had to be so*. Still, there seemed to be no vehicle for both giving expression to that vision and also providing the means to bring it about – until Cell Church arrived! I am not saying that this vision can not be worked out at all in any other church. It can, and the values and principles outlined in this book can be taken into any situation. However, I do believe that Cell Church has provided a unique and wonderful vessel for this new wine!

It is always tempting to want to know how to do something quickly, but the most effective and thorough ways often involve moving slowly. If you have little or no concept of Cell Church then I advise you to read the books recommended in the Bibliography on page 83, as they are the platform on which this book stands. The explanation of Cell Church in Chapter 1 of this book is not sufficient to prepare you to change, or make the *transition*, into Cell Church, but it will give you some basic idea of what it entails.

If you are already a cell church or looking to go that way, then may I plead with you to read through this book prayerfully and carefully, and perhaps attend or hold a seminar on intergenerational cells where the practical outworking can be seen. Do not be tempted to read 'how' and ignore 'why' the wind of the Spirit of God is sweeping through this vision. It is the 'why' that births vision. What is happening is not limited to this country, it is happening across the nations and across every kind of church.

- Where are your children in relation to the rest of the church? Are Sunday School and children's ministry seen as the only way forward for them?

Could there be another way, where they give and receive with adults and young people ?

- Where are your youth? Is all their vitality isolated from the rest of the church?

- Where are the elderly? Is their wealth of experience and wisdom made available to the other generations?

- Where are you? Are you within a generational flow of blessing or are you isolated in 'adult church'?

There is a way to include each of these groups fully.

In the intergenerational cell, everyone (adults, young people and children)
- meets with Christ, as He is at the centre of everything that is said and done.
- receives from Christ, as He ministers to us.
- learns from Him.
- builds up the others, in faith and love.
- develops in their relationship with Jesus and with the other members of the cell.
- reaches out to the lost for whom Jesus died.
- is a giver.
- is able to minister.
- is able to serve.
- is able to pray.
- is equipped.
- equips another.
- takes a full part
- applies the Word of God to their life and so becomes a hearer and a doer.

If this sounds too good to be true, do not dismiss it as such. In my own church, Ely Christian Fellowship, and in many others, this is being walked out. *It can happen* and when it does, returning to our individual peer groups as our main source of fellowship and edification seems like unthinkable! In the intergenerational cell *children* participate and minister, giving to adults and receiving from them; *young people* are trained and released into leadership of cells where their aim is to reach their lost generation; *adults* grow, support, receive from and give to the generations around them. The curse of the divided generations is broken and everyone can be released into the blessing that God intended the generations to be to each other.

Jesus is returning. We are part of the bride He is returning for. Let's prepare for His coming together 'that we may be one', adults, children and young people together for the Son of God!

Chapter 1

The Cell Church

Before we begin to look at intergenerational cells it is important to understand a little of the context in which we are talking. As previously mentioned there are many books written about Cell Church, some of which are listed in the bibliography at the back of this book. A cell church is a church which is made up of cells (or small groups) which are themselves the expression of Church, the body of Christ, and are central to the life of the church. Church, as most of us have known it, has as its focal point the Sunday meeting when the whole church gathers for worship. The Cell Church has as the central focus of its life the individual cell, with a celebration meeting as the coming together of the cells. The following is a brief outline which I hope will provoke you to investigate further if the concept is new to you.

God is doing a new thing across the earth . . . and yet He is doing a very old thing! That is our God! To-day, in nations right across the world, churches are changing to Cell Church. This is happening in many denominations and streams, in churches where there are just a few people gathering together and in those where there are thousands. This is not an adaptation of what we already know in our traditional structures, but a *transformation* of the Body of Christ as she prepares for the coming of her Bridegroom. It involves a *renewing* of minds, values, and lifestyle, not just a change of structure. This change takes time, and churches know that they are entering into a process called *transitioning* that will take about five years to work through.

Cell Church is both inward and outward looking, the quality of relationships in the cell giving expression to Jesus' prayer that we should be 'one, even as I and the Father are one' (John 17), but, at the same time, cell members are in a war together to claim back those who are lost to Jesus.

Community is the essence of who God is. He is Father, Son and Holy Spirit perfectly one – communing together, flowing together and enjoying one another. So community is necessary to know and experience God. *Each cell is community,* not because people live together all the time, but because their lives are a spontaneous flow of relationship, the climax of which is when they all meet together for a weekly cell meeting. Ephesians 2:21 says, '. . . in Him you too are being built together to become a dwelling in which God lives by His Spirit'.

Jesus enlarged his basic family community (His own human family) to include His spiritual family as we see in Mark 3:34: '. . . then He looked at those seated in a circle around Him and said, "Here are My mother and My brothers"'. Intergenerational cells do just that. The Cell Church with inter-generational cells *does not deny* the human family but *opens it up* to include the spiritual family into which we have been 'born again'. As this happens our love for each other becomes a witness to those who are lost around us. John 13:34 says, 'all men will know that you are My disciples, if you love one another'.

A good way to begin to understand Cell Church is to compare it with the biological cell. Just as without cells the human body would not exist, so in Cell Church the cell is the basic unit of the Church and the cells come together for celebrations and larger events. However, these larger events do not take precedence over the cell and its relationships.

The health of the individual biological cells is vital to the health of the whole body! Just as the human body is dependent on the health of each cell, so it is in the Cell Church. The cells are the living organism of the church, a basic community that has within it everything necessary for life. Without the cells the Church would almost cease to exist!

Out of each cell will flow

Figure 1

In order for that to happen central midweek programmes, such as Bible studies, visiting, and training, are removed. This enables the cell to be the *primary focus* of every believer, and allows these elements to become a part of each cell. Removing many central programmes also gives cell members time to develop a lifestyle of community with each other which is not just for their own benefit but also reaches the lost. *Nothing* in the church programme will conflict with the relationships and activities of the cell!

Cell is not just a meeting but a way of life. Cell leaders care for the members of the cell and encourage them to discover and be released into their gifts and callings. These cell leaders are *facilitators* who are always prayerfully looking to see how the rest of the cell can rise to their full potential. It is amazing how leaders emerge who could never previously be seen as having leadership qualities.

The cell meets all together weekly for praise and worship, to focus on evangelism, and to apply the Bible to their own lives. This time together is not about having a Bible 'study' but it is a time where the cell members look into the Word of God, asking the Holy Spirit to bring revelation about changes that need to be made in their hearts, minds and lifestyle. This is very challenging!

In the New Testament we see that Church life was centred around the homes of the believers. In Acts 2:46b '. . . they broke bread in their homes and ate together with glad and sincere hearts'. In a similar way the cell meeting is held in the homes of the different members, each member in turn opening their home, so the meeting place changes from week to week. This takes the meeting of the people of God out into the streets where they live and can impact on their families and neighbourhood.

So we can see that there are distinct differences between the Church with small groups or cells, and the Cell Church. In the former each programme has its own leadership team and clientele, so each meeting may have different people attending and different people leading. With this inconsistency the focus on *relationship* is minimal, with the *meeting or programme* itself being the primary focus.

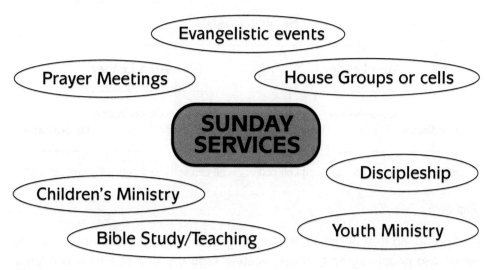

Figure 2

As we have previously seen, in the Cell Church the cell is a powerful expression of Church from which these entities flow (see Figure 1). Members always meet under the same leadership and with the same people, so *relationship* becomes a primary focus.

In most churches as we know them the pastor and senior leadership are the focus with the members empowering them to lead. In the Cell Church, the senior leadership empowers and serves the cell, so that 'the work of the ministry' can really be undertaken by the majority, not the minority.

Multiplication is a natural process in the life of a biological cell, and so it is with the Cell Church. Each cell grows to about 12-15 members, then multiplies to become two cells of seven or eight members each. New leaders are continually being raised up in the cell ready for the time of multiplication. So cells are always looking to reach out to the lost, to grow and multiply to extend the kingdom of God, from the homes of the people who are part of that cell.

As relationships develop, so people become relationally accountable to each other and this is another feature of Cell Church. Members become friends and within that friendship agree to be accountable to each other. Cell leaders in training look to their cell leaders, who in turn are in friendship with their coordinators, and so on. They encourage, help each other, have fun together and pray for one another. As the key is relationship, accountability is no longer seen as a threat to be avoided but is seen as an opportunity to receive help and encouragement. It is no longer a feature of the fear of authority which has threatened the Church in the past.

The following diagram is a brief overview of the structure of Ely Christian Fellowship. (This is a typical structure of a cell church, though titles may vary. Each 'Senior' leader and their family is also in a cell.)

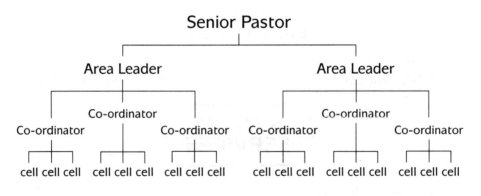

Figure 3

Sponsoring relationships are a key to growth within the cell. Sponsoring is when two people agree to meet together regularly, one of whom is often a new believer. It is a time during which believers are equipped in their walk with God, giving opportunity for personal ministry and sharing. By using materials that are available to help (see Appendix 2) they explore the Word of God and its effect on their lives. In this sponsoring relationship members can grow from the early days of the Christian life on to greater maturity.

Although the cells are the main focus, the whole church celebration is also vital for cell members. They come together for powerful praise and worship, teaching and preaching, to be a potent witness in the locality!

Other events that may take place within the larger gathering of cells are evangelistic or 'harvest events' which serve the cells in reaching their unsaved friends. All large group events within the Cell Church will serve the cell, and not conflict with or distract from the cell or the relationships within it. Consequently the church calendar will reflect this priority.

This is a brief summary of the Cell Church, and anyone looking at this for the first time should read other literature available for a greater understanding (see Bibliography, page 83).

So where do intergenerational cells fit in all this? The answer is simple – all of the above relates to children, young people and adults! Intergenerational cells are primarily where the value of the generations flowing together and appreciating, honouring and loving one another are written on people's hearts. This is manifest by the cells welcoming, including and mobilising members from different generations, including children. In the intergenerational cell Jesus is the centre of a community where each person whatever their age has their own place and their own unique contribution to make. (See Psalm 78:1-7)

A pastor said to me once, 'Daphne, we have always known that this should be the way, but there has never been a model, or anyone to tell us how'. This book is about why and how! It is vitally important to know why everyone, including the children, needs to be included in our cells, why we need each other, and to know why God ordained the generations to flow together. The outworking will then come from our hearts and when the problems arise (and they surely will) you will still be utterly sure that this is the way that God intended for you!

Chapter 2

_ The Intergenerational Vision _

The biblical foundations

> My prayer is not for them alone. I pray also for those who will believe in Me
> through their message so that all of them may be one, Father, just as you are
> in Me and I am in you. May they also be in us so that the world may believe
> that you have sent Me. I have given them the glory that you gave me that they
> may be one as we are one. (John 17:20-22)

This well-known prayer of Jesus has been used in many situations in recent
years, particularly with reference to unity across the denominations, but how
many have thought that this could apply to the generations, as well as the
denominations?

I am convinced that this prayer is being fulfilled in a new and remarkable
way. I see an exciting move of God as the generations are being reunited
and the generational blessing is being restored to the body of Christ. Psalm
78:1-6 speaks so powerfully of the flow of blessing that God intended the
generations to be to each other; yet one generation has learned to despise
another, to have little time for another, and to focus on the problems of relating
to one another rather than the benefits. We have so often lived within the
curse of Exodus 20:5 'punishing the children for the sin of the fathers to the
third and fourth generation' rather than the flow of learning, support, experience,
knowledge and love that God intended when He extended the blessing of
Exodus 20:6, 'showing love to a thousand generations of those who love me
and keep my commandments'.

We were created to live within that generational environment, yet we have
moved into the isolation of a peer-orientated society. Sadly, this culture has
invaded the church as we have created peer group departments, albeit so
often with excellence. Today this is changing, and where this change takes
place it is eventually welcomed and embraced by every generation. As I travel
from church to church, from stream to stream, from denomination to denomination, I see a revolution taking place as the generations embrace each other,
realising the deficiency that has been in their lives through the separation.
Repentance and excitement are simultaneously released. How can this be?
Because it is based on the Word of God – a model for us all to see.

As we look into the Scriptures we see in Exodus 16:9 that 'the *whole*
Israelite community was called before the Lord' to give an account of their

grumbling, and in Exodus17:1 we see how the 'entire Israelite community set out' together – every age, every generation, through thick and thin, on a journey together that took forty years. In Numbers 1:53 we see the Levites being put into position so that everyone was protected from 'the wrath'. There is no age selection in these passages! It is often a major revelation when people realise that when words like everyone or all are used in the Bible, or in the church setting, it is actually referring to everyone – men, women, young people and children!

Then, as we look at 2 Chronicles 20:13, when the Moabites, the Ammonites and the Meunites were coming against him, Jehoshaphat proclaimed a fast and the people came to 'seek help from the Lord'. Here was a nation in trouble, a nation in danger. Did they send the men, the adults or a selected few to stand before God? No! In the face of potential national disaster 'all the men of Judah, with their wives and children and little ones, stood there before the Lord' – and when they did, 'the Spirit of the Lord came upon Jahaziel'. Today, how often do we go together and stand before the Lord when there is trouble around, the men, their wives and children and little ones? Are the prayer meetings of our nation selective, or do we come, all the generations together, to seek our God and hear what He has to say? When the wall of Jerusalem was completed and dedicated to God, 'on that day they offered great sacrifices, rejoicing because God had given them great joy. The women and children also rejoiced. The sound of rejoicing in Jerusalem could be heard far away.' (Nehemiah 12:43)

What a heritage, to be actively involved when the deliverance of God was seen, and to be part of such tremendous praise and worship! They had no difficulty in embracing the promises of Ezekiel 37:24-28, that 'they and their children and their children's children will live there forever'. The children knew their heritage because they had been a part of it!

This book is about intergenerational life in the body of Christ. It is deliberately called intergenerational because it is precisely that! It is not just about including children – a very patronising view that adults might adopt. It is not just about families, for there are many who have no family, yet are part of this wonderful flow in which God has set us all. This is about all of us appreciating one another, giving and receiving from the generations around us, without compromise and without losing our identity, that we 'may be one'.

How good and pleasant it is when brothers live together in unity . . . for there the Lord bestows His blessing, even life for evermore! (Psalm 133)

Kings of the earth and all nations, you princes and all rulers on earth, young men and maidens, old men and children. Let them praise the name of the Lord. (Psalm 148:11-13b)

So why will it benefit us as adults to have the children with us, as part of a church lifestyle, and how will it benefit them?

Deuteronomy 6:4-7 is an instruction to the people of Israel:

> Love the Lord your God with all your heart and with all your soul and with all your strength. These commandments . . . are to be upon your hearts. Impress them on your children. Talk about them when you sit at home and when you walk along the road, when you lie down and when you get up.

This, I believe, is the environment in which God intended our children, and ourselves, to learn – within the context of life itself, and in relationship with others.

What we have learned from experience, what we have heard from those whom we love, will be imprinted forever on our hearts as well as in our minds. In Cell Church, God has given us a very precious context in which to live this out. It is into this environment that we can bring all the generations, including the children, to learn as God created us to learn, through teaching, experience and modelling within the context of relationships. God ordained His command to pass from one generation to another not only through formal teaching, but also by being lived out in practice. By specific command, He included the children in this, making it clear in Deuteronomy 12:25 that we have a direct responsibility to our children, '. . . that it may go well with you and your children after you, because you will be doing what is right in the eyes of the Lord'. And in Deuteronomy 29:29 we see that 'the secret things belong to the Lord our God, but the things revealed belong to us and to our children for ever'.

In Joshua 4:4-8; 21-22 the Israelites were told to build a memorial for their children and the generations to come. The nation was being shown by God how to make time and space for the children to ask questions, and how to carry their godly heritage into the generations to come. The children had been a part of the troubles that the nation had experienced, but they were also a part of the victories.

So often people say that they cannot have children present as it would not be appropriate to share problems with them around, and my response is always the same. The children know about the majority of the problems we face and they often feel a sense of responsibility for them. We just like to protect ourselves from the pain of that realisation. How wonderful for the children to see problems resolved, to see how the body of Christ can support, comfort and pray – and then to see the victory! As they grow up they will know that God can do the same for them.

Of course there are times when it would not be appropriate to share some things in front of children, but then that would also be so with some adults! The *whole* nation had experienced the hand of God in the good times and the bad, so God's decree, that 'all the peoples of the earth might know that the hand of the Lord is powerful, and so that you might always fear the Lord', Joshua 4:24, clearly included the children.

The story of the boy Samuel in 1 Samuel 2:18-26; 3, illustrates the inter-action of the generations and the dependence of one generation on another. Samuel needed Eli, and Eli needed Samuel. They had lived together in a trusting and loving relationship that opened the door for the voice of God to be clearly heard and understood, not only by Eli but by all Israel. For 'the Lord was with Samuel as he grew up, and he let none of His words fall to the ground. And all Israel . . . recognised that Samuel was attested as a prophet.' What a time that was, when a child was taught, seen, heard, respected and nurtured in the house of God not just by his peers but by the man of God.

Children learn so much in the family by watching and then doing themselves. God placed them in a natural learning situation – the family! The promise of God to David, 'you shall never fail to have a man to sit before me on the throne of Israel, if only your sons are careful in all they do to walk before me as you have done' (1 Kings 8:25), rested on that; today we call it *modelling*. In other words, God said, 'I want your sons to watch you and do what you do!', and that is still the heart cry of God today: let your children be where you are, let them see what you do and you will find that they will follow you.

This is a challenge to adults: if the children are present with us, what will they see and hear? Maybe it is a challenge that will prove costly, and will cause us to examine our lives very carefully – which must be good for us!

> He who fears the Lord has a secure fortress, and for his children it will be a refuge (Proverbs 14:26).

How often do we see our own characteristics in our children? They have learned from their environment, which is their foundational training ground; they absorb it as naturally as breathing. Can we rise to the challenge this represents to our own lives, for if we 'train a child in the way he should go, . . . when he is old he will not turn from it' (Proverbs 22:6). Are we prepared to be open and vulnerable in the church environment? In the cells, can we share our lives with them so that they know from our modelling what a holy lifestyle looks like? Can they see from our example what it is like to minister, to be ministered to, to serve, to love unconditionally those of every generation?

The truth is that so often we need the children with us, for they are frequently able to show us the way! Jesus told us to become like little children. He did not mean that we should become childish, but have hearts that were open to Him in a childlike way.

> Unless you change and become like little children you will never enter the kingdom of heaven (Matthew 18:3).

How do we know how to become like little children if we do not have the children with us? Maybe we do not have them there because it will require the very thing that Jesus asks of us, to be 'humble like this little child' (Matthew 18:4). Oh! that the church would repent of the attitude that we are above having the children there, or that we only do it because the children need it. No! We need them, too!

Matthew 18:1-14 contains sobering words of Jesus which are worthy of our time, attention and prayer. If we cut the children off from the generations around them, we deprive them of the life flow that God ordained for them. Matthew 19:13-15 provoked a heart cry from Jesus, 'the kingdom of heaven belongs to them'! Not a different kingdom of heaven from ours – there is only one kingdom of heaven and we are in it together!

When are children ready to start being with us and responding? In the womb. 'When Elizabeth heard Mary's greeting, the baby leaped in her womb' (Luke 1:41). They can be prophesied over even before they are conceived.

> Your wife Elizabeth will bear you a son, and you are to give him the name John. He will be a joy and delight to you and many will rejoice because of his birth (Luke 1:13, 15).

> The child [Jesus] grew and became strong; He was filled with wisdom and the grace of God was upon Him (Luke 2:40).

And where did He live that out? In the community of which he was a part (see Luke 2:41-44). And who recognised that grace and wisdom on His life? Adults!

> They found Him . . . sitting among the teachers . . . Everyone who heard Him was amazed at His understanding and His answers (Luke 2:46-47).

Acts 2:38-39 tells clearly that repentance, baptism, forgiveness, and the Holy Spirit are available for us *all*, for 'you and your children'. Let's enjoy kingdom life *together*. This is the time that was spoken of in Malachi 4:5-6:

> See, I will send you the prophet Elijah before that great and dreadful day of the Lord comes. He will turn the hearts of the fathers to their children, and the hearts of the children to their fathers.

A year ago an eleven-year-old girl we know had a dream. She saw people eating fruit from some trees. It was good fruit and people enjoyed it. Was this not the outpouring of the Spirit across the earth that has refreshed our lives and churches? Then she saw them move on and trees with things like rubber gloves caught in their hair as they passed by – and have so many of us not experienced tough times following that anointing? She then saw big fruit, bigger than before, that people enjoyed – are we not waiting to taste that fruit of revival? And then she saw people holding hands, adults and children going home together: shall we start that journey now?

Envisioning the Church

In the previous section I have outlined a little of the heart of God and His vision for unity within His body. However, we have often had more than one vision within the local Church, one for the adults, one for the youth and one for the children. A scattered vision will result in a scattered people, whereas a single vision results in such power and unity that nothing can stand in the way! Proverbs 29:18 (AV) states, 'where there is no vision the people perish', so where there *is* vision the people, adults, youth and children, will flourish!

In restoring the unity of the generations there must be one vision within the Church; two visions mean division! And that vision must always be to bring glory to God. In this present age what glory will be given to God as the Church allows the Spirit of God to restore, heal and unite us all, for 'by this all men will know that you are my disciples, if you love one another' (John 13:35).

However, vision must be fuelled by faith, and that faith founded on the Word of God, carried, imparted, preached, taught and modelled by the pastor. It is not uncommon for pastors to say that they will send children's workers to my seminars, or to talk to me. But it is the pastor who is the leader; he is the one the people will follow. This vision involves a change of values and thinking that will ultimately lead to changes in the structure of the church. Unless the vision is clear, the people will be confused and so it needs to be carefully shared with adults, young people and children alike; not the vision of a change of structure, but of the values that underlie it. This is why the first part of this book is about values and vision, because problems will come, but the vision will cause you to hold on and press through the problems.

Values always give the 'why', while structure gives the 'how'. When people understand 'why' then the structure will be so much easier to implement. Understanding will give them the opportunity to make their own decisions. Vision produces values, not an imposed structure. Unless the values of the intergenerational cell are thoroughly internalised, the result will be just another programme. The foundation must be found in the Word of God and in the values that are the life flow of His Spirit. Out of that will come the structures. If they are implemented without faith and vision, the intergenerational cell will become just another idea.

God gives us the vision, then he takes us down to the valley to alter us into the shape of the vision, and it is in the valley that so many of us faint and give way. Every vision will be made real if we have patience. *Oswald Chambers*

When looking to implement the intergenerational cell the first thing that needs to be asked is whether the senior pastor has caught the vision. Is he prepared to enter into the lifestyle and eventually be a member, not a leader, of an intergenerational cell himself? His example is vital; he is the leader in word and deed. When he has caught the vision and heard clearly from God, then he is ready to impart the vision to the Church by preaching, teaching and sharing the vision. Ideally this is done in small groups where people can discuss and ask questions.

I cannot offer the hope that this will be without risk, for risk is a natural part of growth and change. It is a natural part of moving into the vision and cannot be avoided. Before long the pastor will see who has caught the vision and who will run quickly into it. These are the people who can model it to the rest of the church, as they translate the vision into practical outworking. Perhaps one cell at first, a prototype cell, might take the intergenerational values and live them out in the cell. As others see it working, so the vision will spread, both through the multiplication of the cell and through being caught by others wanting to run with it. Good news travels fast! While the vision will not be birthed in consensus, it will result in consensus as people watch and walk into it. It is all right for others to follow more slowly.

When a cell has been modelled successfully, no one can say that it cannot be done, and everyone has somewhere where they can experience it. It is vision! Experience will speak far louder than many hours of talking. In the pioneering stage, if a children's worker leads the first cell, the assumption will be that special skills are needed. If possible, during the early stages of establishing intergenerational cells, have leaders who are totally committed to the vision, but would be seen by the Church as the most unlikely candidates to lead a cell with children in! The truth is that the only skills needed are those related to running a cell, not skills specific to children.

Please print the following indelibly on your mind and heart; it is a simple fact but one of the most profound that I can impart to you: most of the problems experienced with children, probably 95 per cent of them, are to do with the mismanagement of the cell, or a lack of the vision and values of Cell Church, not to do with there being children present.

Another group of people who will need to understand clearly the values that underlie the changes are parents. They need a place where they can be encouraged to ask questions and receive answers based on values. It is vital to involve the parents, to maintain their parental responsibilities, and build trust. When a parent is envisioned the child always benefits.

Then it is imperative to envision the children's workers. Their role will inevitably change. The children will be pastored by their intergenerational cell leader, to whom children's workers will need to submit their pastoral responsibility. However, the children's workers need to impart cell values to the children, giving them a clear vision of what God is doing, always promoting the cell as their primary focus, and taking an active interest in their cell life.

Vision is given by God to His Church through the heart of the pastor. Vision is given by God to the cells. Vision is given by God to *all* His people. The vision, fuelled by faith and prayer, will transcend our minds and produce such faith in our hearts that it will become reality. How do I know that God wants to restore the flow and blessing from generation to generation within our churches? Because it is decreed in the Word of God. How will you know that it is possible? Because the Holy Spirit will write it in your hearts as He has in mine and you, too, will know that, despite what you see around you, God has made a way to heal His body.

I said to the Lord not long ago, 'Lord, I want to see miracles. I want to be used by you to heal those who are sick,' and He said to me, 'I am using you to heal the sick. I am using you for miracles. I am using you to heal my broken body'. That is my vision.

He will speak to you and give you vision. If you are a pastor, ask God for personal vision, then ask for vision for your church, so that you can impart it to your people – all of them, all the generations. God will always take you from where you are to where He wants you, if you allow Him to do so.

I have lived for years with the vision of an intergenerational life within the body of Christ, but it has seemed like having new wine with no wineskin to put it in. Cell, I believe, is the wineskin! However, I could not be released into it until I was in a place where the pastors of my Church were convicted by the Spirit of God that this is, and always has been, His plan for His people.

So I would reiterate what has already been said: 'Pastors need to carry, impart, teach and preach the vision'.

When leaders lead in Israel, when the people willingly offer themselves, bless the Lord! (Judges 5:2, New King James)

Changing our world view

The intergenerational cell will gradually change the world view of everyone in it. We have all related to God in a way that has been filtered through the environment in which we were nurtured, that is, our family of origin. Our character, values and relationships are a result of that family environment. As none of us was born into the perfect family, we all had parents who were not everything that God intended them to be. As a result we are all damaged, some more than others, but nevertheless we all need healing.

Our souls reflect their feelings onto God. How important it is, therefore, for our souls to be healed! Here is a simple exercise that will help you to discover how true this is: write a list of the things that you 'know' about the character of God, then write a list of the things that you 'feel' about God. Perhaps the first list says, 'loving, just, merciful, trustworthy, faithful' and suchlike, while the second says, 'distant, not sure if He understands me, or whether He loves me as much when I sin as when I minister for Him' and so on. The differences are born out of our relationships with our childhood family environment. We all need restoration in our souls, and cell is a place where that restoration can take place. It will not be easy; change never is, but it will be possible.

Teaching alone will not heal us. We were born within relationships and so will change within a relational environment. As the cell gives people the opportunity to develop godly relationships, their relationship with God and man will be affected, and their souls restored.

> How can a man (woman or child) love God who he has not seen if he has not been loved by man who he can see? *Paul Hegstrom*

Cell is not just about meetings, it is about ongoing relationships. It is a place where many of our problems can be worked through and overcome. We would consider it foolish to try and ride a bike on ice, or use a computer in a steamy bathroom, as neither would operate effectively because they were never intended to work in that environment. Yet we have tried to live out kingdom principles in the church in a totally different environment from the one in which God created us to be. We have tried to 'ride a bike on ice' and wondered why we did not achieve all that we hoped for!

In a functional family everyone is valued for who they are, and so it is in a functional cell. *Everyone* is valued. How many adults or children know, see and feel that they are valued just for who they are within the church to-day? How many of them know, see and feel that they are valued by other generations? How many know, see and feel that they are valued by God for who they are and not according to how they perform? The intergenerational cell is the place where this can start to happen, where men, women, young people and children can find their family of God and therefore begin to experience more of the character of their heavenly Father.

How can we move into the intergenerational cell from a situation where we have often kept other generations at a distance? First, let me state that cell principles are cell principles. We are *not* looking to find different ones for an intergenerational cell; what we are wanting to do is to involve everyone.

In many of the situations in which people live, at home, work or church, there is a tendency towards a very *self* conscious attitude. The first consideration in most things is, 'How do *I* feel about this?' 'What do *I* want?' This creates an environment where masks are worn to protect from rejection, conflict is left unresolved, forgiveness is earned, and acceptance based on performance. How can this be challenged? How can we move to a new place?

When people become part of a cell they are challenged because the opportunities for hiding begin to disappear as Jesus is allowed to be the very centre of the cell. As the focus moves from 'me' to 'Jesus', relationships must also change until forgiveness becomes a gift, and people can acknowledge their feelings without having to hide, because they recognise that they are valued and can trust the other cell members, so they feel safe. Within the environment where the love of Jesus is the bond and motivation, it becomes possible to resolve conflicts.

This presents a challenge for change to every person, every generation and every family. When God gives us vision, it is by the Spirit of God that we are taken step by step into it. Moving into intergenerational cells is moving against the kingdom of darkness. The enemy has taken ground by robbing us of the flow from generation to generation, almost without the church as a whole being aware of it. He will quietly hold on to this ground unless we, by the power of the Spirit of the living God, move against him. This is spiritual warfare!

Where families have been separated, the cell provides a re-creation of family where everyone has their own unique place, yet all learn to live with godly values together. Today many are isolated from their own family, and many have no family at all. If people are privileged to be in a situation where this is not so, then they have something precious to share with those who are not so fortunate. Whatever our situation, we need each other to give to and to receive from.

Parents today often feel unable to cope with the demands of parenthood, and feel isolated in those responsibilities. In addressing this problem the answer in the church has often been to relieve the parents of the pressures by physically taking the children to another place. The cell is an environment where parents can be empowered, where experience is available, where one can learn from another, and each cell member supports parents who are struggling. Some parents feel ashamed of their children's behaviour and this has kept them from the church. Cell is a safe environment in which to address the problems together. None of us has all the answers, but between us, as a body, we can act together with godly wisdom. In societies where the generational lines have remained intact, parents have support from the other members of the wider family; however, in our society so many families are fragmented generationally that this lifeline has been broken. What an opportunity for support and restoration within the family of God!

Family life continues in the intergenerational cell; everyone is involved, and the unity of the family is preserved. The interaction between cell members becomes a lifestyle which involves everyone, and the family can continue the interaction at home with shared vision, shared experiences and shared community. Parents are able to see and encourage their children as they develop their gifts in the cell and the home. Instead of fragmentation, there is an inclusive flow between cell and home.

The pressure of material things, rejection by friends and family and abuse in its varied forms are leaving a trail of destruction in the lives of Christians and non-Christians alike. There is a heart cry within every person for acceptance and healing. So many adults are looking for families, men and women looking for the fathers they never had, children denied the daily input of fathers. Cell is where there are 'fathers for the fatherless'. The community of the cell is a God-given environment where healing can come through relationship.

When God created the family He wanted an expression of Himself; He wanted His image to be reproduced in unity and harmony. God Himself is community, Father, Son and Holy Spirit, relationally communing and flowing together. When God created Adam and Eve, He wanted a reflection of Himself. Had they not sinned, Adam and Eve's family would have been the community with which God would have lived and felt at home. How exciting to be able to be part of a move of God, where God Himself can feel at home! As we allow Him to recreate that image in the cell, as we receive, by faith, the gift of community among us, our churches will experience healing and we will again live in the environment in which we were created to live.

When God set His people Israel in order, he placed each individual within a family, each family within a tribe, and each tribe within the nation. No generation was excluded, no child left out, no older person put aside. Within each tribe were the components of family: they were community.

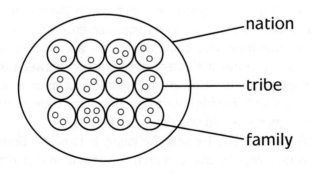

Figure 4. Family, tribe and nation

Now God is bringing that same order back to His people. As churches throughout the world move into cell, so His community is being restored as God originally ordained! Each family within a cell, each cell within a congregation.

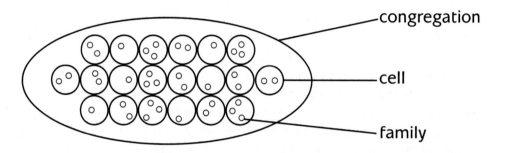

congregation

cell

family

Figure 5. Family, cell and congregation

Where young people and children grow up with strong relationships, having others in their lives besides the nuclear family, they build a storehouse for the rest of their lives. They were never intended by God to be divorced from the community environment or from the input of both older and younger generations. Many are wounded because they are so heavily influenced by their peers, who are struggling themselves. I am not denying the fact that we need peer relationships, or that these should be strong and are of tremendous value, but they need to develop within the context of a strong family, or community, base. This base provides resources to draw on, opinions to consult, people who will pray. How essential that children and young people are nurtured in the body of Christ with those strong godly influences, among people who will love and accept both them and their family! When we started to impart to the church the vision of the restoration of God's plan for us to flow together, we did not hurry to integrate the 15-25 year olds. However, it was not long before *they* came to ask *us* why we were not giving them older people to meet with, and to tell us that they liked younger children! We then acted quickly, as they felt that they were being deprived – and so they were!

Good questions that reveal the extent of interaction between the generations in a church are, to adults, 'How many children and youth in your church would you really call your friends?' or to children and young people, 'How many adults in the church would you really call friends?'

In Psalm 68:6 we read that 'He sets the lonely in families'. Sometimes we have read that as meaning the whole church congregation is one family. This can scarcely ever be true, because a family should be small enough for you to feel special and loved. The cell can provide that environment as it embraces 'the solitary'. Solitariness is isolation and isolation robs the individual of friendship and others of relationship with them. God is a relational God, we are His body, we are relational people. He made us to be that way. There are too many lonely people in the body of Christ and they need family!

Why are the elderly so often not included with the young? Why are children denied their heritage? Some of the most mutually precious experiences are those of the interaction between the young and the old. Here the stories of the wonders of God are being passed from generation to generation, wisdom and experience living with energy and innocence. No wonder the devil has kept our eyes veiled from seeing what he has stolen from society and how he has infiltrated wrong values into so many churches. We have generations in conflict and yet we avoid the resolution of that conflict. The intergenerational cell is the place where the conflict can be safely addressed, the curse broken, and the blessing taken hold of.

So many believe that we cannot worship together, cannot have fun together, and that the children 'get in the way'. Adults often appear not to be interested in receiving from children, and the elderly are often quietly put out of sight like the children. Somewhere in our spirits we have known this is not as it should be.

We must wake up, take back the blessing of the generations together, no matter what the cost – and there will be cost! No war is fought, no territory regained without it. Leaving the familiar, good or bad, is often hard, particularly when it requires changes in lifestyle and new paradigms – but Jesus is coming for His bride, for a people prepared. He created us perfectly and we can do no better than return to His original plan.

Chapter 3

_____ Children (and Adults) _____

'As with adults'

This simple statement can make including the children easy.

Children have the same needs as adults in many areas of their lives. Most of the problems that are encountered are because their needs are expected to be totally different and adults then feel that they could never cope with any significant interaction with them. This expectation also results in children behaving in an appropriate manner. Sometimes people come and say that they were in one of my seminars, so I ask them to prove it. They reply, 'As with adults!', and I know they have been. I shall now ask the same thing if you tell me that you have read this book!

At the basic intergenerational cell seminar we have a brainstorming session on what an adult would want from church. The response is always varied, but the replies include:

- to meet with Jesus;
- fun;
- friends;
- people who will pray with and for me;
- encouragement.

Then we look at the list and ask how many of these things a child would _not_ want. Always it is possible to say that the child would want the same thing, so it is 'as with adults!'

You will notice time after time in this book that when children are mentioned, in brackets afterwards it says 'as with adults'. I am not simplistically saying that this is true of every situation, but remembering this will certainly help you find the answer to most of the difficulties you might encounter.

The following list has an element of fun, and, as you read it, you will see a principle which is very liberating to those who think that they would not possibly know what to do with a child!

Welcome the children (as with adults)
- It is the children's cell meeting, not their social time . . . as with adults.
- Alter your vocabulary, do not use long words or religious language . . . most adults will understand better and so will those new to the kingdom of God.
- Do not move on without checking the children have understood . . . you need to do this for adults, too.

- Children have a range of understanding . . . as with adults.
- Keep a check to ensure no child is excluded . . . as with adults.
- Check that children are included in conversation and interaction, or they will get bored and lose interest . . . as with adults.
- If the children are bored, look at what is going on. Is it creative, relevant, inclusive? . . . as with adults.
- Follow up the children's comments; treat their input seriously . . . as with adults.
- Ask for their opinions and ideas . . . as with adults.
- Follow up any problems they may have . . . as with adults.
- Check they are not sitting too closely together . . . as with some adults!
- Draw them out . . . as with adults.
- Have expectations and standards relevant to their age, for example, no crawling on the floor during the meeting . . . as with adults!
- Support, encourage and follow up the children . . . as with adults.
- You may find it hard to accommodate some children . . . you may find it hard to accommodate some adults. Prayer and relationship will find the answer for both.

What do children receive from adults?

Children see their parents as all-powerful and believe that they are 'god-like'. The truth is that they were intended to be God-like, the filter through which children could catch a glimpse of their heavenly Father.

In infancy there is no separation between children and their mother. As the years pass, both parents are the world through which they live and they begin to see through their eyes, speak their language, and adopt their values. The parents are the child's world.

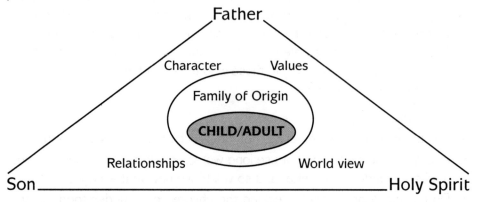

Figure 6. How do children see God?

Their parents are so powerful to them that if things go wrong, or even feel wrong, they will believe that it is their failing not the parent's, that they are to blame and must therefore be unlovable. For example, if children are being valued only for their achievements, they will feel that, if they fail to reach a standard which is beyond them, they will become unlovable. Consequently their view of God will be that they must perform to win the love of their heavenly Father. If things are not right in their world, then they will feel it is their fault, which will carry guilt and shame into their relationship with their heavenly Father. Children are not able to separate these experiences out and very many adults in the body of Christ are still trying to disentangle themselves from this confusion in their lives.

In the light of this we see that, in order to transform the world of children, we must touch the world of parents. There have been many wonderful ways of reaching children and of drawing *them* into the kingdom, and I have been a part of these. They are valid and powerful but, unless we reach families and draw *them* into the kingdom of God, children will be left in an ungodly environment, and still see the kingdom of God and their heavenly Father through that filter.

The environment of the intergenerational cell offers the potential for healing of the whole family. Therapy today is offered in the context of the family recognising that everyone is important if change is to be effective, and that the interaction of family members is a vital part of that healing. We need to hold on to that wisdom, for it is as God intended it to be, the children and parents together 'working out their salvation with fear and trembling'.

Unconverted parents of children who are saved may be won for Christ through cell friendship evangelism (see *Sowing, Reaping, Keeping* by Lawrence Singlehurst). By the power of the Holy Spirit, and with the support of the cell, their lives can be transformed, along with those of their children and the generations to come. What a privilege, to touch the lives of parents, change the world of a child, and impact generations! Do not underestimate what happens when parents' lives are changed and when a child's life is touched and transformed. When you look at a child, you can see the generations that will come as a result of that child. Influence a child and you touch a new generation.

It is a tremendous privilege to touch the life of a child. Babies are born literally naked in every way, ready to receive unconditional love, expecting their needs to be met and to fall totally in love with their parents. That is how God created them. The problem arises because, when man fell, the devil was well aware of that vulnerability and chose to use it for himself. The result is that unprotected, vulnerable babies and children have been harmed by the imperfections of a fallen world. However, they are still like putty, and God is a

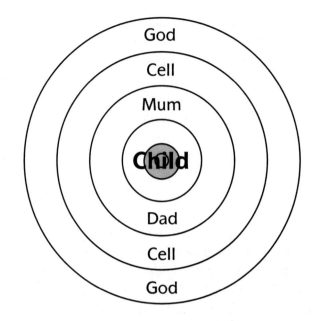

Figure 7. How do children see God?

redeemer whose heart's desire is for that vulnerability to be made available to Him through His people. When we touch the lives of children we can so easily leave imprints on their lives, for good or ill. While many are emotionally and physically hurt daily, both in and outside the body of Christ, let us treat the opportunity to be a part of that redemption through the intergenerational cell as an honour.

Children, young people and adults live out the messages they receive from others. What message are we giving to them in our churches? Did you know that psychologists say that 7 per cent of what a child, or adult, receives will be from the words spoken and 93 per cent will be from the tone of voice and body language. Mixed messages are received when there is conflict between the spoken words and the actions that go with them. 'Of course I love you', spoken impatiently, has little real meaning!

Here are some examples of the mixed messages that so many churches send to children:

Words . . . 'You are a valuable member of the church.'
Action . . . We give you no opportunity to minister to us.

Words . . . 'Jesus loves your worship and praise.'
Action . . . We can worship better without you around.

Words . . . 'You can move in the gifts of the spirit.'
Action . . . You can do this with other children, not with us.

Words . . . 'It is important that you come to church.'
Action . . . We give you no ownership, you are a spectator.

Words . . . 'We go to church as a family, because that is important.'
Action . . . We go our own ways when we get there, and do different things.

A child said to me one day,
    'We all went out together as a family last week.'
    'That is wonderful,' I replied, 'where did you go?'
    'We went to the cinema.'
    'And what did you see?'
    'I saw *w*, Mummy saw *x*, my brother saw *y*, and Daddy saw *z*.'
    I was unsure how to respond, as this child saw a family outing as going to a multi-screen cinema with everyone watching a completely different film, sitting in different rooms. Then I began to think, 'Isn't this what we do with church when we say that we go as a family?'
    Even if the parents disciple their children, the body of Christ still needs to do its part. Where relationship is concerned, the Sunday school often offers an orphanage environment. It tells children that they can receive all they need from a few adults who see them occasionally, having little personal interaction with them on a day-to-day basis; the rest of the time they can receive from their peers. There are many excellent Sunday school programmes, many Sunday schools that offer children so much, but they are mostly detached from the vision of the Church and the prayer life of the Church, and the interaction between adults and children is very limited. The main thrust of the Church takes place in a different location, with different speakers, teaching a different message from the ones that the youth and children are hearing.
    As a result, children often visit the body of Christ and receive very little in relationship terms to counteract all that they face in the world.
    The intergenerational cell affirms, in deed, the words that are spoken:

The words say . . . 'You are a valuable member of the church.'
The intergenerational cell says . . . 'We want to receive ministry from you.'

The words say . . . 'Jesus loves your worship and praise.'
The intergenerational cell says . . . 'We love to share in worship with you.'

The words say . . . 'You can move in the gifts of the spirit.'
The intergenerational cell says . . . 'We receive the Spirit of God in you, and recognise gifts He has given you.'

The words say . . . 'It is important that you come to church.'
The intergenerational cell says . . . 'The cell is yours as much as ours.'

The words say . . . 'We go to church as a family because that is important.'
The intergenerational cell says . . . 'Our families are part of the wider family of
the cell.'

From this we see that children, like adults, need to receive at the deepest
level the message out of which we want them to live. This will change their
experience and their actions, and they will receive a clear message of the
kingdom of God. Children will live out of the messages they receive in childhood
for the rest of their lives. Let's give them something wonderful to live out of!
What are we giving the children? How can we pour into their lives something
that will last for ever, something that will stand in the storm, something that
becomes a part of them?

What are we giving the children?

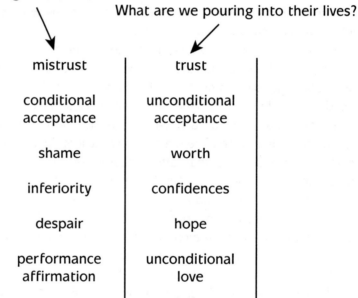

What are we pouring into their lives?

mistrust	trust
conditional acceptance	unconditional acceptance
shame	worth
inferiority	confidences
despair	hope
performance affirmation	unconditional love

Figure 8

Only a lifestyle relationship can offer the positive in a lasting way because it
is lived out in words and deeds, in situations that are relevant to daily life as
seen in Deuteronomy 6:4–9:

> Hear, O Israel: The Lord our God, the Lord is one. Love the Lord your God
> with all your heart and with all your soul and with all your strength. These
> commandments that I give you today are to be upon your hearts. Impress
> them on your children. Talk about them when you sit at home and when you
> walk along the road, when you lie down and when you get up. Tie them as
> symbols on your hands and bind them on your foreheads. Write them on the
> door-frames of your houses and on your gates.

As we look at the lives of so many adults, we see them living out of all that they received in their childhood – mistrust, shame, inferiority, despair and a drive to be accepted through what they do. What a privilege to have an environment where that can change for them, where the generational curse can be broken, and where they and our children can learn trust, and receive unconditional acceptance, worth, hope and confidence from what they hear and from what they experience. When we begin to understand the impact that we can have on a child and understand how our own misconceptions and misbeliefs can impair their spiritual growth, then we begin to understand the importance of asking the Holy Spirit to renew our hearts and minds in these areas, and make us more like Jesus.

God created the child, He created the development of the child, He knows the perfect environment for the child to be nurtured in and for His perfect plan he ordained FAMILY.

What do children (and adults) believe?

What do many children, and adults, still generally believe? I am not talking about what they might say they believe, but about what they believe in their hearts. Much of what we say we believe has been imparted through teaching, preaching and reading. These things are valid and necessary for all of us; however, unless there are times when what we have been taught is put into practice and seen to be relevant, it will not have the same transforming power. This is called *experiential* learning.

I am using the word *believe* here to mean *being utterly sure,* to the point where my belief becomes something I live out of, and influences every area of my life. So let's look at what children believe, bearing in mind that much of this still applies to many adults too.

Generally speaking, children believe that God does not directly affect their lives unless they are specifically shown His hand at work on their behalf and can see the evidence of His love for them in their lives and the lives of others around them. They see Him as God who controls the weather, or has control over events like earthquakes, aeroplane crashes and other disasters. Unless they are in a good interpersonal environment, they continue to believe that God sees and knows everything in an impersonal way. They need personal interaction with people who know them well enough to be able to show them the evidence of His guiding hand in their daily walk, at home, at school, in the cell or at play. Then they can come to know Jesus as their shepherd who knows them personally, who counts the hairs on their head, calls them by name and meets their needs. If the members of the body of Christ have no intimate knowledge of the children, how do they know, in a way that is written on their hearts, that God has?

Many children, and adults, believe that God operates rather like a magician, that He has 'powers' that He can use in a very impersonal way. They see Him rather like their 'invisible' friends, until they discover that His power works for them, and they did not create Him! When children and adults together begin to discover the wonder-working power of a creative God who responds within personal relationships, then they are ready to release that power to others, and to have faith for God to release His creative power into their lives. They begin to have faith to be healed and for their needs to be met – in fact, when they see God's power at work, they accept it completely, and their faith is so powerful that, if adults deprive themselves of the presence and input of the children, they are the losers indeed!

Sadly, the Bible is a book that children, and adults, often feel is too hard for them to understand, and irrelevant to their lives. For that attitude to change they need guidance and help to relate to the Bible personally. It is a sad fact that, when they do hear the word of God, they are challenged in that moment, but that is all. God becomes just the God of the Bible until they actually start to live out of it, and to believe that, just as God delivered Daniel, so He will deliver them; just as He welcomed children into His arms, so He will welcome them. Children (and adults) have so many questions, things that they need to ask to make the Bible make sense and be relevant to them. They need to be able to ask those questions and receive answers.

It is the outworking of a personal relationship with the Almighty God that changes lives, and God gave us His body through which we would experience His love. Children believe wrongly that God is very far away, but the truth is, God is a God who speaks to them. All they need is for people to help them identify His voice, rather like Eli did for Samuel. Then they will know that He is very near, very interested in them and has a relationship with them that is eternal.

Just as Samuel would have watched Eli and learned so much from following and imitating him, so children (and adults) need to be able to watch others. We do that all the time. We see television advertisements, we see the way others dress, talk and relate. From our earliest days we learn to live out of those things. Originally, God wanted to write on the hearts of children as they watched their parents. Today He still wants to write on the hearts of children (and adults) as they watch, imitate and learn kingdom living. This is the most natural way of learning, of growing and changing. It is important that the cell members realise this, for we *will* learn from each other, which brings with it a very challenging responsibility. Maybe we don't want to assume that responsibility in front of our children! It is worth reiterating that, when we begin to understand the impact that we can have on children, and understand how our own misconceptions and misbeliefs can impair their spiritual growth, then we can begin to understand the importance of asking the Holy Spirit to renew our hearts and minds in these areas and make us more like Jesus.

The children's (and adults') misbelief, that God is an event God who is available at Christmas, on Sundays or in prayer times, will disappear as they are supported in living out a daily interaction with their friend, the Lord Jesus Christ!

How did God ordain these needs to be met? Where did He want His children to become acquainted with Him? Where did He know that they would have their lives forever imprinted with His heart? Within the context of relationship, in an informal life-related environment. It is called family, or community. It could be called the *intergenerational cell*! Why does the cell meet these and other needs in such a very special way? Because children (and adults) are included in a meaningful way, they do not see it as a place that is mostly for adults, where they have no say in what happens. Instead of feeling that they have nothing significant to contribute, they are given ownership in the same way as adults and their input is valued and respected. Instead of being in a setting where adults give and they receive, children find that they are in an environment where adults are open to receive from them as well as to give to them. Instead of feeling they must wait until they are older to discover their gifts and callings, they find that these are recognised and encouraged. Many adults, too, have so much to give yet have not had a place where this is recognised. For them, too, the cell is a place of security and of opportunity to explore and exercise their gifts.

In the intergenerational cell everyone can realise their potential, not in a separate building, not just among their peers, but in the context of Church, in family, in the community that He has created! Here they can move into a relationship with Jesus and His people. Through that relationship they will discover that Jesus really is 'the same yesterday, today and for ever', and know that they are loved, appreciated and valued.

Experiential learning is a process we all come through, a natural learning process in the context of family. The Church has called itself a family but has not recognised its role in the development of the members of that family. The good news is that, through the intergenerational cell, we can create the informal, life-related environment where what we believe will be written on the hearts of the children (and adults) through sharing our lives with each other, under godly authority with love and care.

Summary

Children believe that God does not directly affect their lives **unless** they are shown His hand at work on their behalf.

Children believe that God sees and knows everything in an impersonal way **unless** they find Jesus as their shepherd.

Children believe that God is a magician
unless they discover the wonder-working power of a creative God.

Children believe that God controls the weather and allows accidents
unless they see His guiding hand in their daily walk (at school, at home and so on).

Children believe that God is just the God of the Bible
unless they live it out; for example, God delivered Daniel, He'll deliver me, too.

Children believe that the Bible is too hard for children and irrelevant to them
unless they are guided and helped to relate to it personally (in words they understand).

Children believe that God is like their invisible friends
unless they discover that His power works for them, not their power creating Him.

Children believe that God is very far away
unless they learn to hear His voice.

Children believe that God is an event God (prayer times, Christmas, Sundays)
unless they see the daily interaction of God in their lives.

Children believe that Church is mostly for adults
unless they are included in a meaningful way.

Children believe that they have no say in what happens in the church
unless they are given some ownership.

Children believe that they have nothing significant to contribute
unless their input is valued and respected.

Children believe that they are always the receivers in church
unless adults are open to receiving ministry from them.

Children believe that they must wait until they are older to discover their gifts and callings
unless their gifts and callings are recognised and encouraged.

What do children (and adults) need?

Children have needs, so many of them just the same as ours, needs of a childhood many of us have long forgotten. To summarise some of the things that we have already addressed, children need:

- to know that God is present and to see the evidence in their own lives.
- to experience the reality of God for themselves.
- constantly to discover more of God.
- to know people care about them as individuals.
- to relate to others and be related to.
- to know that it matters that they are present.
- to be recognised, included and understood.
- to be given ownership and appropriate responsibility.
- to see their own value.

   However, there are some issues which need to be addressed further.

Children need safety and protection

An intergenerational cell does not put children at more risk because they are exposed to more adults; on the contrary, it offers greater protection. Parents maintain their oversight and responsibility at all times. As in normal family life, their children are not removed from them without their permission and they are far more aware of their child than in church situations, where they may have no idea what the children have been taught, how they behaved, how God used them or what their struggles were. In the cell parents are encouraged and enabled to make decisions and maintain their responsibility. When they need and want it, they can also be given support and help from other cell members, not necessarily other parents, as many single people miss having children of their own and love to be involved with them.

   Having said that, it is necessary for every Church to have a child protection policy that is clearly understood by cell leaders, all those in positions of authority, and as far as possible by every member. Help with formulating this policy can be obtained from the local child protection officer at the police station, who will give ongoing advice to churches and other organisations involved with children.

   Accountability within a framework of friendship is a strong feature of the Cell Church. A significant distinction is made between *secrecy*, which says, 'I will tell no one', and *confidentiality*, which says, 'I reserve the right to tell those to whom I am accountable'. This provides safety and security for the children.

   It is important not to allow the devil any foothold and sensible precautions, such as not permitting a child to be taken into a closed room alone with one adult, are necessary to protect the adults from false accusations, as well as for the protection of the children.

Children need to be recognised as individuals. (So do adults!)

Children have their own personalities, their own unique contributions, their own problems, their own achievements and joys. They also have their own relationship with God. They, too, are on fire for Him at times, then find the fire has almost gone out at other times. They, too, need to be encouraged and ministered to when they fall away from God. They need to be supported in prayer and to be discipled. They need someone who sees where they are at and lovingly takes them on from that place, encouraging them to grow in their love for Jesus and to receive His love. Too often children have been grouped together on the assumption that they are all at the same stage in their relationship with Jesus. In fact, as with all areas of their lives, they are each developing spiritually at their own unique pace, which is not age related, but relationship related. As this is recognised and understood, so they will be able to receive the relevant encouragement and help to enable them to grow as Christians.

Children and young people need to have someone in the senior leadership of the Church who ensures they are never forgotten when decisions are being made. This does not mean that the children are included in everything! In the church there is often the assumption that children will not be included, whereas in the family, when decisions are made, everyone's needs are addressed. In family situations sometimes we decide to take the children, at other times parents decide to have some time alone. There are times when children like their own space, or young people ask for time on their own, but it is not a decision made by default. The whole family acts together to support the decision and make the necessary adjustments.

So it is in the cell. We remember that we are family; adults support the children as they spend time together. At other times, the adults may decide to have some time alone, and the children understand this. Young people enjoy their peer groups and are supported in this. However, these are considered decisions, and not part of a lifestyle that ignores the needs of certain members of the family, as can happen in many churches. So, having someone on the decision-making body of the church who always asks about the children and young people when decisions are being made is essential.

Children need to be children. (Adults need to be adults!)

We do not want to impose adulthood on children; we are not trying to make them what they are not. Rather, we are wanting to release them into their childhood, so they can experience its joy, and so we can look on and bask in the joy, too. We want childhood to be important and recognised, children to be included and released. They have far more potential than is appreciated and their exuberance, faith and simplicity are often the catalysts that lift cells into life, and out of many of the pitfalls that adults slip into when they meet together.

It has been interesting to see how, when cells eventually include children, they can no longer remain passive but are challenged by the openness of the children, which introduces a spontaneity and freshness which was lacking before.

Children need to pretend and copy

This is one of the ways they learn. They do it all the time in their family, so why does it seem such a terrible thing when they do it in the family of God? Why should anyone think it is all right when children pretend to be parents, or school teachers, yet mind when they pretend to be praying, or lifting their hands and copying what others are doing in the cell? Children need role models and I praise God that the intergenerational cell gives children the opportunity to copy and then move into the experience. Is that not what many adults do?

So it is fine for children to copy and do what their parents are doing in cell, at church. That is the way they learn everything else. God created us to be in families so we could watch and experience what we were going to move into. The same is true in the family of God. In the intergenerational cell, children have the benefit and privilege of an extended 'family', of seeing others who have strengths that their parents may not have. They can copy whatever they see going on, because their parents are doing it and because they see others too! This benefits adults as well; they need to see *how*, and then *do* also!

Children need to test their environment

Children feel secure within clear boundaries. They need to know what is permitted and what is not. (So do adults!) Testing is a part of finding out whether the environment is safe. Every child is happiest when they can experience unconditional love and acceptance with godly discipline. For many parents, cell is a place where they can discover what effective and loving discipline looks like for their child.

How do children (and adults) learn?

The cell is where children (and adults) learn as one learns in a family, within an environment of love and acceptance, rather than in a school situation. Our foundational learning, our value system, our modelling is all imparted through our families. That is where we learn and change almost without realising.

If the word *teaching* is mentioned within the context of the church, it is commonly related to how much Bible study is going on and at what depth. Whilst that is important, teaching is far more than that. In the cell the focus is on applying the Word of God to our own lives, from which no generation is exempt. When that is happening, we are all in the same position. As the Word of God is opened in the cell meeting, every person, young and old, is asking themselves how it applies to them and to the situations they face every day, at home, at school, at work, at play.

As cell members share their lives together, sponsor each other and move into accountability relationships, so they build strong relationships as 'iron sharpens iron' and lives are changed. Cell members (adults and children) are looking for a change in their values, in their lifestyle and relationships with God and man, not just an accumulation of knowledge.

In the cell children (and adults) learn through:
- watching each other.
- questioning and finding answers to things that have troubled them.
- experiencing community within the body of Jesus.
- receiving guidance from leaders and other members alike.
- helping others, for no one is unable to help another. Far more is learned from 'giving' than we could ever imagine.
- failing. This is a good way to learn, but people only dare to put themselves in a situation where they might fail if there is a measure of trust and security, and the assurance that help and encouragement are at hand to try again.
- succeeding, for they then come to a place where they know they can move on to the next challenge!
- applying the Word of God to their own lives, for this is the very foundation upon which all the above rests.
- seeing others and their walk with God, for they see the Holy Spirit powerfully at work in the body of Christ.

This 'seeing' is not a passive experience, which would not produce effective change or effective learning, but an active experience, of which the children are a part. Consequently, all the following are excellent ways for the children (and adults) to learn. In cell they see new believers on fire in their 'first love' for God, and can capture the excitement; they see people fail and learn to love and pray for them instead of judging or criticising. Gradually they experience the forgiveness and unconditional love of God as it is expressed through His people. More importantly, they learn that they are a part of the expression of that love. They learn to accept people as they are, and see that they, too, are accepted just as they are. They see that it is acceptable for everyone to grow at their own pace, as within the family.

As they live in an environment where everyone is accepted just as they are, and is helped by the power of the Holy Spirit to grow towards maturity, so they will find the security to do the same. They see people dealing with problems in different ways and working them through and understand that God is a personal God who relates to individuals and does not work by formulae. They see that problems are victories in disguise and can relate that to their own lives. As they observe others facing problems and are included in praying for them, so their own faith grows. As their own problems are taken seriously by members of the cell, so they begin to see that 'what He's done for others, He'll do for you!'

They see older believers secure in their relationship with God and know that, if they continue in their walk with God, they too can experience that depth of relationship with Jesus. How wonderful for our children to have 'heros' who walk with God, who reach out to them, using their influence for good in the child's life, and to have a community within the body of Christ where 'learning' is a continual path that can transform every part of a child's, or adult's, life!

Once we let go of our old ideas of what *teaching* means, so much of what happens in cell assumes a new importance.

Chapter 4

_____ The Cell Meeting _____

Structure

It is important to remember that the cell meeting is not the whole life of the cell. At the meeting the community comes together as *a part* of the lifestyle that exists between adults and children. It is a focal point where everyone meets with their Lord Jesus Christ, who is at the centre of the meeting, changing lives and bonding relationships together in His love.

Adults so often have lost the sense of fun, spontaneity, challenge and creativity that brings life to the cell meeting, so having children present can prevent it sinking into an intensity that brings death, not life! The children can inspire and enthuse adults in a very special way. We need them with us and children need older people to empower and recognise them, since unless adults include and honour them, they cannot be released into the place God has for them in the body. Adults can either quench or welcome the children in the cell meeting. Most children will respond positively if adults take the initiative.

We are surrounded by a hurting and lost world. Jesus never advocated that our lives together should be introspective and selfish, so it is from the security of the cell that adults and children are able to reach out to the lost with mutual support and accountability.

Just as the human cell is made to multiply for the growth of the body, so the church cell is made to do the same. To facilitate that growth, the meeting needs a structure that is easy to reproduce. The meeting then becomes a place for gifts and ministries to emerge in adults, young people and children. Multiplication also requires new leadership to be constantly being raised up. By seeing every member, whether young or old, as a potential leader, cell leaders in training are easily identified.

For all this to happen the cell meeting needs a skeleton or framework. The human skeleton is basically the same universally – that is how the human form is recognised. However, each person is very different from the next, having their own unique characteristics and identity. So it is with the cell meeting; the skeleton is essentially the same, but on that 'hang' the differences between the various cells, and even between the different meetings in any one particular cell.

While every church may have a core of members who could facilitate a cell quite easily, that will not promote growth. However, when there is a structure that is familiar and that has been seen to be effectively modelled, then virtually anyone can be responsible for parts of it.

One of the reasons that our cell meetings are prepared centrally is so that they can easily be given to leaders to delegate to their members. Most of our cell leaders are now very grateful that they do not have to spend hours in preparation.

Each person takes responsibility for a part of the meeting, or for part of the cell life, for one series (seven or eight weeks). This enables them to develop in that particular area, particularly if they are given appropriate help. When responsibilities are given for one week only, people do not have the opportunity to improve or to take ownership in the same way.

All our cells use the same outline material in any given week, but I can attend several different cell meetings in one week and find each one having a new anointing, and a fresh identity. Those members who are creative and able will develop the material further, those who have never taken any responsibility of this nature before have something that empowers them.

It is so exciting to see children and adults flourish in areas in which they have never before been equipped to succeed! Many start off falteringly but, with the encouragement, faith and prayer of the cell, they develop and grow.

How often have we seen leaders 'burn out' under the weight of responsibility? Shared responsibility and ownership gives people confidence to become Aarons and Hurs.

Another reason why all the cells have the same material given to them is that we are moving as one. When the Church of God moves in unity it is effective. Some objections to this commonly raised are:

• *We may feel led to do something different.*

The Holy Spirit leads the Church under the authority of the pastors. If they know that He wants to speak to the Church about a certain subject then we need to trust them and God in this! Would we decide to *do something different* in a celebration, when the pastor had made a request? No! The pastor does not stop pastoring the Church when the cell meeting starts!

• *We feel the need for our cell to address certain issues.*

Remember that there are seven days in the week and six other nights when the cell can meet to do whatever they please!

• *The Holy Spirit needs to be able to move.*

He does, in an amazing way, where leaders walk humbly before God and those in godly authority over them. I have seen lives change and felt the anointing of the Holy Spirit strongly in meeting after meeting where people have obediently done everything they have been asked to do.

• *Isn't it restrictive?*

No, it is liberating! Those who are able develop the basic material in wonderful ways. Those who are not so able are free to take part because they have something they can handle and make their own. Leaders are free to spend their time praying and discipling their cell members instead of planning.

Having an underlying structure also ensures that every cell receives a 'balanced diet'. A leader who loves worship will want to spend longer in worship, another who has a heart for evangelism will want to see the lost saved above everything else and therefore spend longer on evangelism, while yet another might prefer to spend longer in prayer. All leaders have their own strengths and weaknesses. The given skeleton ensures that each cell will be offering a balance at each meeting, so that each person present has the opportunity for 'healthy growth'.

The purpose of the cell meeting is for adults and children to develop within the values of cell, which are

- love God
- love each other
- love the lost

and is primarily for edifying and discipling Christians in their relationships with God and man.

Non-Christians are best invited to the actual cell meeting once they are open to the Gospel, and have already had the opportunity of meeting cell members in social settings. This way, when they eventually attend the meeting, they will meet a group of friends, and a God, to whom they have already been introduced.

The four Ws

Having described the significance and value of a common basic structure, let me introduce you to the 'skeleton'. This is what is commonly known within Cell Church as the four Ws – Welcome, Worship, Word and Witness.

The meeting flows almost imperceptibly through these parts:

- Welcome, which includes the icebreaker
- Worship, including the offering
- Word, the ministry of, and finally
- Witness.

The maximum time from the start to the end of the meeting should never exceed two hours. (In some places this time is very much shorter and can be as little as an hour.) This is really important as meetings that go on beyond the expected finishing time leave people feeling insecure and parents can feel very vulnerable when children's bedtimes are imminent.

When a new group is formed, for a few weeks more time will be spent in the Welcome, then in the succeeding weeks time in the Worship and Word will increase until later, as the cell prepares for multiplication, more emphasis is placed on the Witness. All the components need to be present throughout the cycle.

A suggested average timing would be 30 minutes for the Welcome and icebreaker, 15 minutes for Worship and the offering, 25 minutes for the Word, with an extra 15 minutes for ministry, and 20 minutes for the Witness. Sets of meeting outlines, which include guidelines for each section of the cell meeting, are available and details are given in Appendix 2.

The following gives an overview of what could be contained in each of these sections. Notice particularly the tips for including the children which are in italics.

1. Welcome

This is the time when the group is arriving at the home where the meeting is being hosted. Each home should be visited in turn and a hosting schedule is used to ensure that this is planned well in advance. Some people may resist the meeting being held in their home. There is always a reason for this and it is essential gently to discover and address what underlies their reluctance to open their home. Every member is important and every home acceptable!

Be sure to put children's names on the hosting schedule on a separate night from their parents. They love to open the door, serve drinks and feel it is 'their' night. They may need help with this – but then some adults may need help too!

A drink may be provided as people chat informally. Take care that there is no segregation at this time. *Children should not be allowed to run around the host home, or disappear off to play together. It is their time to get to know other people by talking with them, and gives others the opportunity to get to know them.*

The *Icebreaker* gives everyone the chance to take part and speak at the very beginning of the meeting. One person is responsible for bringing the icebreaker question, which can be casually informative. These questions are not designed for very intimate sharing, but to give everyone the opportunity to say something and to get to know each other better. They start the meeting in a very relaxed way. Examples of icebreakers would be

- 'What was the best thing that happened to you this week?'
- 'If you could fulfil any ambition what would it be, and why?'
- 'If you could win one person to Jesus tomorrow, who would it be and why?'

The question is asked by the adult or child responsible for bringing it, and that person answers it first, which models the time to be spent and the flavour of the answer. It is then passed around the group in rotation. If the question was not prepared centrally, always check with the person responsible before the day of the meeting to be sure it is an appropriate one.

Children love to take part, and to be responsible for the icebreaker. After they have seen it modelled they find it easy to lead, even if they are very small. When homes are hosting where small children are about to go to bed, they often see it as a great treat to be allowed to stay up long enough to enjoy the icebreaker and worship before saying 'good night' to their cell members.

2. Worship

This is the time to remember that Jesus is at the very centre of everything the cell does. Although the worship is brief, it is the time when we welcome the Holy Spirit, and recognise our dependence on Him.

Be creative! Singing songs is only one way to worship. They are valid contributions to this time, but be sure to choose songs that do not have too many different verses. This allows both adults and children to enter in without the effort of continually focusing on different words.

However, if singing is the only expression of worship, then people will feel that only singers can lead this time. Our aim should be that everyone can lead, so here are a few ideas – there are many more!

- Read a psalm, or create one together.
- Bring different items, hand them round, and ask people if they remind them of anything for which they can thank God.
- Take a tape, listen to a song and then join in praising God as the song ministers.
- Sing responsively.
- Encourage people to get out of their chairs.
- Place a candle in the middle of the room and ask what the group is reminded of, then read an appropriate scripture while music is playing in the background.
- Let each member look out of the window, then ask them what they saw to be thankful to God for.
- Let everyone say a simple prayer of thanks.
- Encourage kneeling, holding hands, speaking to each other, confessing the Word.
- Use a guitar, tape or sing unaccompanied.
- Experiment with journalling, which is listening to God and writing it down (children learn to do this in the *Living with Jesus* series, details in Appendix 2).

During this time be aware that the Holy Spirit may want to minister through words of knowledge or prophecy, whether through an adult or a child.

Some children will feel more capable of leading this section than others, but the same is true of adults! A child might be paired with someone who is more confident, so that they work together.

Creativity and activity are wonderful in worship. Many times it is the children who will lead the adults out of their armchairs! I have found that groups with children generally have more life in their worship, because everyone enters into it freshly each time. This time is certainly not about singing 'children's' songs. Sing those that minister to everyone and bring people close to Jesus.

The *offering* is a part of worship, so it will flow easily during the worship time. Again, creativity keeps the joy, faith and vibrancy in giving. Use, for example,

- A testimony of God's faithfulness.
- A Scripture.
- A story of God's goodness.
- An article out of a Christian magazine.

Encourage the person responsible to bring their own container for the offering. This may be something that is special to them, or something they have made specially for this time.

Children often have more faith for finances than adults, and their simple words of exhortation can break spiritual strongholds over this area.

Beware! They may bring the most creative offering containers!

3. Word (or Life Application)

This part of the meeting focuses on applying the Word of God to our own lives. It is *not* an academic Bible study! Led by the Holy Spirit, the cell leader will facilitate discussion relevant to the lives and situations of those present, using questions such as

- 'How did that make you feel?'
- 'What would our group be like if we all lived that Scripture?'
- 'What changes do we need to make in our lives if we are going to live that Scripture?'
- 'What do you think God is saying to us right now?'

Materials are included in the meeting outlines (see Appendix 2) that are suitable for all ages, and will facilitate this section. However, if the Word of God is constantly being applied to each person's life in a group where there is trust and openness, then everyone, whatever their age, can take part.

If you have an intergenerational celebration, then the group could share how the message spoke to them. The forms on pages 107 to 109, which we sometimes use in our own celebration, are completed by adults, youth and children during/ after the celebration, then taken to the cell meeting as a reminder. Filling in these forms also helps everyone to focus during the message.

This section is not usually delegated as certain skills are needed to draw everyone out, to prevent domination by any one member and to keep the group focused on the application of the Word. Usually the cell leader will facilitate it, or perhaps the cell leader in training.

We have found children very responsive, and certainly very challenging! As the group honours their input, so they will be more confident in sharing, as with adults! The simplicity of applying the Word of God to our lives is for everyone. It becomes relevant to child and adult alike.

It is important to read a version of the Bible that the children will understand (but then most of the adults will understand better, and so will new believers).

Ministry may flow at any time during the meeting. Occasionally this may be during the worship, but more often it will be appropriate to minister into an area that members have come to the meeting to share or which has been revealed during the Word, or even the Witness section. Sometimes this can be prepared in advance, while at other times the need will be seen spontaneously. It is a precious time when members pray with and for each other. It is not an appropriate time for 'deep' ministry.

Children will automatically enter into ministry once they know that they are actually needed, respected and wanted in that situation.

Once adults release the children to express their faith and operate in the gifts of the Spirit, a new dynamic is released in the meeting which is free from religious constraints and preconceived ideas. A key to that release in ministry is that everyone (adults and children) gives, and everyone receives.

4. Witness

Here we focus on the world in which we live and those around us who need Jesus, those for whom he died. Each week the group may

- share how they are getting on with their friends and assess the response to Jesus and to the friendship being offered (see *Sowing, reaping, keeping,* Lawrence Singlehurst).
- Send a couple out to prayer walk the street where the meeting is taking place.
- Plan social events to which they can invite their unsaved friends.
- Pray for group members who are meeting resistance in their friends.
- Plan to help each other by building friendships with one another's friends.
- Pray for harvest events (larger gatherings, to which the unsaved may be invited) such as seasonal events, productions, parties, dinners, bands or concerts.

During this time everyone can share their personal problems and the challenges that face them as they reach out to the lost around them.

Cell leaders often report that they find this section the hardest to facilitate. It is not surprising that the enemy would want this section omitted. Again, creativity keeps it alive and prayer pulls down strongholds.

Children are more spontaneous in their evangelism than we are, but face the same disappointments that we do. They need us to empower them. We can plan children's parties to which they can invite their friends. We can reach families if we take our children with us to their homes. Children love to prayer walk and they will take an interest in your friends if you include them.

The intergenerational cell provides a unique opportunity for children's evangelism, because, as children reach out to their friends, there is a whole network of support and prayer to propel them forward, protected and empowered. As they reach their friends, adults reach out to the parents in friendship.

An example

The following is a brief outline of an intergenerational cell meeting that actually took place. Although it is very brief, it gives a flavour of the interaction.

Welcome and Icebreaker – Matthew, aged 8 years.
Matthew's icebreaker question was, 'If you could be any part of a car, what would it be and why?'

His answer was 'I'd be a horn because I wake everyone up!'

He then passed the question around the circle, letting each member answer in turn.

Worship – Tony, aged 12 years.
Tony read a short psalm, then asked people to read it in different versions. He then led the singing of *Lord, I lift your name on high* several times through.

The cell leader then said, 'Let's stretch our hands to the centre of the room and feel the presence of Jesus. He is at the centre of our meeting and at the centre of everything we do and everything we are.' Pause and pray.

'Now let's put our left hand on the person beside us and pray for them to feel the presence of Jesus tonight.' Pause and pray.

'Now let's stretch our hands to the world outside and pray that people out there will know the presence of Jesus.' Pause and pray.

Offering – David, aged 9 years.
David read Psalm 67. He then exhorted us always to bring an offering of praise to God, whether it includes money or not. He passed an offering tin around with a robot from *Star Wars* on the top and then prayed over the offering.

Word – Cell leader.
The cell leader read Matthew 26:69-75 dramatically, then asked, 'Have you ever known that you should have told someone about Jesus but didn't do so?' Nearly everyone shared. We then discussed these questions:

- How did you feel at the time?
- How do you think Peter felt when asked if he knew Jesus?
- How do you think he felt when he went out and cried?
- How do you feel about the times you did not speak up for Jesus?

The cell leader suggested that we close our eyes and quietly tell Jesus how we felt, and ask Him to forgive us. (There followed a time of repentance.)

- When Jesus looked at Peter, what do you think His look said?

Ministry – Cell leader.
The leader asked Phil (an adult) to go round every member, look into each person's eyes and tell them what he thought Jesus would say to them. (There followed a very moving time of simple, edifying prophetic words spoken to each one.)

Tony then gave Phil a word for himself.

Witness – Margaret (an adult).
Two people from the group left and went to prayer walk the street where the meeting was being held.

Margaret then said, 'Let's pray in pairs for the people we are reaching out to'. When this was done, the group then called each one in by name, for example, 'James, come into the kingdom of God'.

Chapter 5

_____ The Cell in Practice _____

Tips for leaders

Preparation

Always prayerfully prepare well in advance of the cell meeting. This preparation should include the cell leaders and cell leaders in training all meeting to pray together.

Where materials are given to cell leaders in advance, it is important that the cell leaders allow the Holy Spirit to challenge their own lives as they prepare. If the Holy Spirit has already spoken beforehand, the leader will find flowing with Him far easier in the meeting. Leading without constant reference to the sheets of paper is vital.

Another essential part of the preparation is to check that each person who is going to lead a part of the meeting has also prepared well beforehand. They may need help or 'coaching' during the early weeks of responsibility. Although the cell leader is ultimately responsible, the person who had the task (or ministry) for the previous season could oversee the next person for a few weeks. This is good training, teaching each one to raise up another. Another essential element of raising each person in ministry is to give relevant feedback after the meeting. This should always be edifying, while at the same time giving them opportunity to improve.

It is good to spend time with the coordinator and other cell leaders praying over the coming meetings and sharing creative ideas. Our cell leaders meet with the leadership monthly and part of that time is spent envisioning them about the coming series of cell meetings.

A series of forms is provided in Appendix 3 to help leaders to organise their meetings and report back to their coordinators. You are welcome to photocopy these for your own use, or just browse and get ideas from them.

Leader's role

In our church each series usually consists of seven weekly meetings, the first one always envisioning the cell members about the coming series, praying about it and handing out responsibilities; four cell meetings on a specific theme; one evening with welcome, worship and prayer, and one week when the cell has a social outreach event, specifically focusing on people they are reaching out to.

The cell leaders are both facilitators and participating members of the meeting. Both of these roles are vital to the success of the meeting. As facilitators it is important to

- keep the focus off themselves, so developing and encouraging interaction between all the members.
- notice those (adults, young people and children) who have not contributed and draw them out.
- keep a healthy balance of interaction in the meeting between the different age groups and personalities.

Every leader will take time to develop these skills whilst maintaining a quiet authority.

The other role, that of being an active member of the group, will, incidentally, also help facilitating. Becoming vulnerable, sharing and allowing others to minister, models the way forward to the group. So many leaders wear the mask of leadership and suffer under the strain that it imposes on them. Cell leaders are also people with needs and, within the context of cell, can be seen and known for who they really are; they too can have their needs met.

Bible reading

Decide which version of the Bible the cell leader is going to use in the meetings. While children, young people and adults will each bring the version they are comfortable with, it is important that leaders use one that most people will understand. Always read Scripture in a lively and meaningful way – the cell will see that this brings life, and, when asked to read, will do the same. Wherever possible, ask two or three different age groups to read from their own version. This will ensure that everyone hears the word freshly several times.

Small groups

During the meeting it is good to break into smaller groups. This may be during the *Witness,* for prayer or ministry, or for parts of the *Word* section. It is useful to do this at any appropriate time for closer interaction, but this strategy will be of particular help when:

- the group is getting larger.
- there are problem people who can monopolise the whole meeting (this localises the problem).
- the group is not responding as a whole.
- the group is looking to the leader to provide all the answers.
- there are people who are holding back from participating.
- it is important that everyone has an opportunity to give or receive.

If smaller groups are used during the *Word* section it is good to feed back to the whole group so maintaining unity and allowing the whole group to be able to hear how God has moved amongst them all. This feedback, however, need only be very brief.

Feelings

Questions about feelings are important for everyone – adults, young people and children. Everyone has feelings! Feelings are good and acceptable and are not to be judged, because they need to be owned by people. However, they do drive behaviour, so how we behave is often determined by what we feel. When applying the Word of God, it is important for everyone to look at the roots of their behaviour. Consequently, being real and identifying feelings is important and challenging for all ages. It brings repentance, vulnerability, encouragement, and revelation.

Modelling

Always 'model' the meeting for a season before distributing the responsibilities. Remembering that one of the most effective ways of learning is by seeing, experiencing and doing, or 'modelling', it is essential that members of the cell have a good experience of an intergenerational cell meeting before they are given responsibilities within it. When satisfied that the group has seen good timekeeping, the four Ws effectively facilitated within the flow of the Holy Spirit, creativity and all members effectively included, when they have seen prayerful preparation, then it is time gradually to release others into responsibility.

Hosting

Encourage people to check that the room in which they will host the meeting is free from toys and other things that might be the ultimate temptation for children (young people and adults)! A sheet thrown over certain items, like computers, will be adequate. Arrange seating before people arrive, making sure everyone can see and be seen.

Encouraging

Should children need encouraging, small rewards work wonders, so long as they are given in a meaningful way and every child has the opportunity of obtaining one. I would recommend that these are given from time to time, keeping the element of surprise alive. When given every week, they eventually lose their significance. Our church is strong in the belief that most things are 'as with adults': I have known cells who have given incentives to everyone who has participated. This element of fun has produced breakthrough for adults and children alike!

The children belong to the whole cell. Show the adults how they can offer positive encouragement to the children as they sit with an adult, for example by saying, 'Would you like to help me? I like the ideas you have', or 'I've saved you a space as I want to hear all about . . .' This allows each child to be helped, should they need it, makes sure they are integrated and prevents the temptations that arise when they sit in a block together. (You may recognise that this is the same with some adults!)

The Kids' Slot

What is a Kids' Slot?

I would like to share what we in Ely Christian Fellowship have done to include our children to the fullest extent. This is a personal testimony, not directive advice!

The majority of our children stay in for the whole of the cell meeting, and we find their contributions are invaluable.

A Kids' Slot is when children or adults go to another room for the *Word* and the *Witness* sections of the meeting, so that the children have a time that is totally child-orientated.

In our church a Kids' Slot is not seen as a permanent situation, but one which works towards the child(ren) being able to take their place with the rest of the group when they are ready.

This is *never* introduced as a negative experience, or a punishment, and there have never been problems about taking children into the Kids' Slot, or with those left in with the adults; everyone is recognised as growing at their own pace. *So* . . . some of the options are:

- A Kids' Slot for all children every week.
- Start with a Kids' Slot when the cell is formed and introduce the children as they and the others are ready.
- Be versatile and have a Kids' Slot for children who would find it difficult in the meeting . . . many children relate better among adults, while others find it hard.

Every cell member has the privilege of being on a rota to take the Kids' Slot time with the children. Remember that the children belong to all the cell, not to a few selected people. Each one will need to see the Kids' Slot modelled by someone who is confident and then have the opportunity to ask questions both before and after the meeting. Those less confident could take it with another group member for a season.

One of the aims of this time is to focus on the children's relationship with Jesus, as well as them getting to know each other and the responsible adult. Children love to hear personal stories about adults, especially about their childhood, so it is good to encourage this as well as listening to them!

It is not imperative to know all the answers to the questions the children might have; 'I'll find out and tell you on . . .' is quite sufficient. Though be sure that you do follow through!

At an agreed time, the children return to where the adults have been and both groups share briefly how God moved among them. This is often a powerful time of sharing – it is not just for showing drawings!

It is *really* important that each person facilitating this time comes prepared, having spent time praying for the children and themselves. If members understand some of the values outlined in this book, they will understand that it is indeed a privilege to take the Kids' Slot.

The children's co-ordinator

One of the responsibilities of the cell will be to have a children's co-ordinator whose responsibility it will be to

- organise a rota of members to take the Kids' Slot (possibly in pairs).
- check that each home has a place to hold the Kids' Slot (a bedroom, large kitchen, hallway).
- collect any relevant materials and ensure each person has them a week in advance, so that they have time to ask any questions they may have about them.
- organise a book for each person to complete, putting in it anything that needs following through, problems that need addressing, prayer requests and encouragements, or tips for the next week.
- take a sheet, or a large piece of cloth, to each home! This is an invaluable piece of equipment to cover anything in the room that might be a distraction to the children.
- report and talk through any problems with the cell leader, keeping the cell leader informed about the children's progress.

If a cell is having problems with one or several children, the first thing that happens is that a co-ordinator visits. Most of the time the problem is because the cell is not being facilitated as it should and therefore *the children are only highlighting the presence of a problem.* In that instance there needs to be some adjustment for the benefit of everyone and the children can be 'thanked' for revealing this. The following are some examples of this:

- One cell did not give responsibilities to everyone, including the children, so the children did not feel that it was really their cell. When they had responsibility, and therefore felt valued, their behaviour changed. It was a cell problem, not a children problem!
- Another cell was too large, everyone was having problems.
- One cell was being very uncreative . . . it was dull for everyone!

If the co-ordinator, or children's co-ordinator, has visited and sees that there are age- or behaviour-related problems that need working through, then a 'Kids' Slot' is introduced for the child(ren) concerned.

What happens in a Kids' Slot?

This may vary from church to church though the following are ideas from which you may draw. Never forget that the aim is for the children to grow as they are empowered to love God, love one another, and love those who are lost to Jesus.

Before the children leave the room it is a good idea to pray for them and then let them pray for the adults. This creates a sense of excitement about what God is going to do in both groups.

It is possible to take the same questions and theme as the adults are using. These will already have some creativity but it may be appropriate to introduce some more. For example, when the cells were looking at temptation, one of the questions was 'What does it feel like for you when you are tempted?' The person taking the Kids' Slot put a dish of sweets in the centre of the room where the children were, then left, closing the door behind her. When she returned every little child knew what temptation felt like! This approach will maintain the same direction for the whole cell.

The *Living with Jesus* series can be used quite effectively, though it is essential to ensure that each child has their own book and a personal follow-up with their 'special friend' or sponsor during the week. Alternatively your church may decide to write its own material.

For the *Witness* part of the meeting the children, too, will pray for and share about their unsaved friends. It is important to keep parents aware of who their children are reaching out to. It may be appropriate at times for the cell to organise children's events specifically to support the evangelism of their children.

The Kids' Slot is about relationship – with each other, with the adult and with Jesus.

Children and young people

In Ely Christian Fellowship most of the youth and children of the Church are in an intergenerational cell which is their primary 'home'. As previously described, they are totally integrated into all areas of the life of the cell. It has been one of our aims to break the mentality that children and young people belong to a department, or select groups of ministers. They belong to the Church and their cell. They are the Church's children and young people!

Changing cell

Until the age of 13 years (the age of accountability) children remain in the same cell as their parents. On their thirteenth birthday they have the option of choosing to go to another intergenerational cell. If they decide that they would like to move to another cell and their parents agree, they talk to their cell leader and then visit other cells. When they have decided where they would like to go they talk to their cell leader who communicates with the new cell leader. Finally they are prayed for by the whole cell and are sent out to the cell they have chosen to join. This is their first opportunity to learn what it means to leave a church in an appropriate way, something that many adults still do not know how to do!

The transfer procedure of the Church is followed so both cell leaders are in agreement, as well as the co-ordinator. I would add that no young person has ever left a cell in rebellion against their parents or other members of the cell. Many do not leave until they are older; some are 15 years of age and still with their family.

We do believe that, during adolescence, young people are finding their own identity and that struggle is often mirrored in their walk with God. Giving them this choice has been empowering and validating for them as they have moved into the adolescent years.

Remember! 'Intergenerational' is a value, not a structure, so wherever the members of an intergenerational cell go, they carry those values with them. When the children and young people go into the world of their peers, they take godly values. They live knowing that they are a part of a redemptive work of God, knowing that they are honoured and loved by all generations. Where so many of their friends will be seeing the generations as an 'enemy', to be fought and not trusted, our youth will have a living testimony to the contrary.

These values cannot be thrust on others, so youth especially need to reach out into their own generation, reaching them at the place where they can be accessed. Adults cannot enter their world at school, they cannot be teenagers again but they can support and pray for the youth of their cell as they reach out to their generation. This principle is true for any member of the intergenerational cell, for each person needs the support and prayers of the rest as they reach out to touch their world.

Youth cells

It is for the express purpose of empowering our young people to reach their generation that we are equipping our youth to lead youth cells. These are peer-led cells which raise up our own young people in leadership.

Each of our youth cell leaders is required to be in an intergenerational cell, where they have taken responsibility and become part of the lifestyle of that community. They attend their intergenerational cell prayer meeting, and receive the support of their cell. Each youth cell leader is responsible for keeping their intergenerational cell informed about the progress of their youth cell, and for taking prayer requests to the intergenerational cell prayer meeting.

There is a leadership structure for the youth cells, with co-ordinators and an area leader (all members of intergenerational cells), who work with the senior leadership team. A part of their task is to maintain their integration into the body and to submit to the pastoring of the intergenerational cell.

On Friday evenings the Lighthouse Centre (the Church building and offices) is open as a youth 'Drop-in Centre', where there is snooker, table tennis and suchlike available. Besides their own personal friendship, this is one of the openings that the young people have to draw others into their cell. Youth rallies and youth celebrations are part of the strategy to empower our young people and reach out to the whole area.

Before launching the youth cells, the leaders, between the ages of 14 and 16 years, were given a few weeks' additional training when they were encouraged to make decisions for themselves, such as organising the groups and deciding standards of leadership conduct.

We used *Cell iT* (see Bibliography) as a basis for training and the early cell meetings though, because our young people had been members of an inter-generational cell for two years, they were already living out many of the cell principles which were part of their lifestyle and experience.

As young people come into the youth cells there is also the opportunity for members of the intergenerational cells to reach out to their families. This is a model that we have adopted within the overall ethos of intergenerational life in the whole of the body of Christ. Other models may show children and youth cells having their separate place in the body, with the youth only being part of a youth cell.

One of the barriers that we have had to bring down is the mentality that the youth (and children) belong to a select group of people – youth workers. Our youth belong to the whole church! The links between the youth cells and intergenerational cells have gone a very long way to breaking that paradigm, but another thing that has helped is that, when our young people spend a couple of hours together on Sunday evenings, an increasing number of adults have opened their homes to them. A rota ensures that the youth now visit many church members. Initially we had a short list of people who offered in fear and trepidation. We had people who opened their homes and disappeared out as quickly as possible, leaving the home to the young people! The climate has changed now; there are many homes open to them and the hosts get involved, get to know them and quite voluntarily give them treats. Comments now are, 'Thank you for the opportunity, we love having them!'

Similarly the young people have learned that they must take their place responsibly in the body, so they set out chairs for a Sunday if they used the church building on a Saturday, they leave homes tidier than when they arrived, and look to bless the adults and children.

Always the focus is, 'What is God wanting to do with us as a Church?' But we also acknowledge that there are specific issues that young people need to address, that they do enjoy each other and need to pull together to reach their generation. We choose to support them pro-actively!

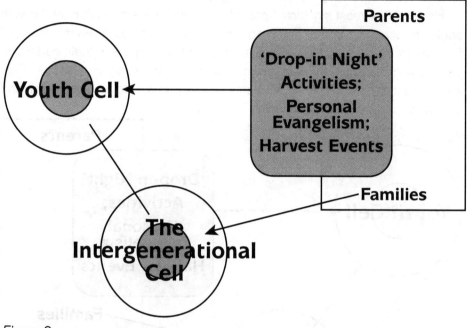

Figure 9

Children's groups

The following is an account of how we have integrated children's groups/cells into an intergenerational Church.

The groups have been implemented because we see them as a tool to raise up our own children in leadership and to reach other children. Ten- or 11-year-old children (school year 6) lead groups of other children of primary school age. These children are also in an intergenerational cell, taking their share of responsibility. They have learned what it is to facilitate, to share ownership, to be accountable and obedient, through the intergenerational cell. They may lack skills but they have a confidence that has been gained from ministering to and with people older than themselves.

The children attend their prayer meeting with their intergenerational cell. They know how to pray and where to bring their prayer requests so that their own intergenerational cell takes an interest in the children's cell they are leading, prays for them and supports them in any way they can.

Before starting their cell each child was given a few weeks' training on subjects like

- What is a leader?
- Confidentiality compared with secrecy.
- What needs to change in my life if others are going to follow me?
- Praying for my group.
- Identifying and bringing down strongholds in my group.

However, the most significant part of this training has been through 'as with adults' involvement in their intergenerational cell. This has given them a solid foundation from which to launch out. The children prepare in their leadership pairs, using materials that are given to them three weekly in advance. They are accountable to one adult, who acts in a similar way to a co-ordinator, and supports them from week to week.

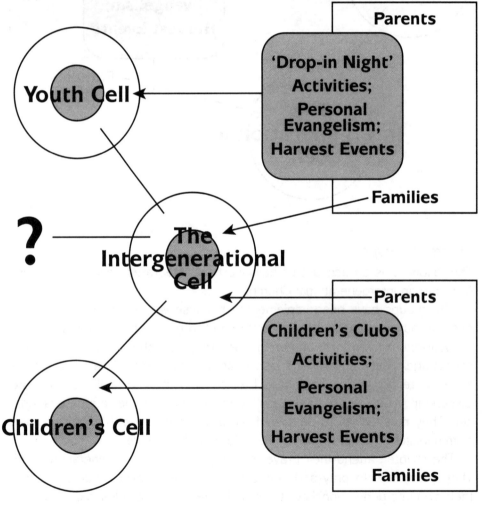

Figure 10

As new children come to the children's cell there develop opportunities to reach out in friendship to the child's family by members of the intergenerational cell.

Discipline

Boundaries are important, loving authority is essential, standards need to be clear, and appropriate behaviour agreed by all, otherwise this can be one of the greatest stumbling blocks in the intergenerational cell. Each family will have different standards and expectations, different ways of disciplining. So . . . the answer is for the cell family to agree together. This agreement needs to include everyone, adults, young people and children. Some things that will need to be considered are

- How do we treat each other's homes?
- How will we talk to and about each other?
- Do we give other members permission lovingly to discipline our children?
- Do the parents want to be told directly about any behavioural problems and have the opportunity of disciplining their own children?
- What is appropriate behaviour in the cell meeting?

It is an idea to have a time when the children go aside and draw up their own guidelines, perhaps under the guidance of an older child who has a list of topics to be considered. At the same time the adults could be considering the same topics. Eventually the two groups could present their ideas, compare them and come to agreement.

I have heard many parents object to taking their child to a cell meeting, claiming that it is their 'night off', or they have 'had enough'. In nearly every instance it has been fear that they will be left alone to cope with what has hitherto been too much for them, or that their children will show them up. However, I have never heard that expressed by a parent who has been lovingly supported within the cell. I believe that within every parent is the desire to have good relationship with their children, and to know how to be successful in parenting; but they have lacked support and modelling.

Does that mean that every cell must have or be a family who has 'got it all together'? It is obviously useful to spread the problems around, to make sure that no cell has an overload of the same type of problem, if that is possible. But the answer is not to be found in any one person, or any one family. The answer is found in Jesus and in His body, corporately.

At this point I would reiterate that when children exhibit behavioural problems it is essential to look at the cell dynamics and to ensure that they are not manifesting a problem that the older members of the cell are quietly putting up with. Remember that children often act out what many adults are only doing inside!

Prayer in the intergenerational cell

Prayer is an essential part of the cell. It is the place where power is released into every person, and every aspect of the cell. It is the place where the cell can reach the nations, change the locality and reach the lost. Everyone (children, young people and adults) can participate in the prayer life of the cell. Our cells have at least one time a week where they meet to pray, some for half an hour before the meeting, others have another time, but they recognise that without prayer they will never be the people God has called them to be.

There are times when you may want to pray without the children, there may be times you want to pray without some of the adults. Do not be age conscious. Some children can cope with more than some adults, some children have an intercessory gift, so look beyond the age barrier that has made incorrect assumptions about the individual's ability to pray effectively. However, it is important that the *whole cell* prays together regularly. Every member needs to grow in their prayer life and there is great power released when the cell comes together in simple unity to pray.

Prayer meetings that are regular but shorter are very effective! Children in our cells attend a weekly half-hour cell prayer meeting. Once within a series the cells also have a prayer evening, when they have the usual welcome, icebreaker and worship, then pray. The children participate for as long as the leader feels they are able; in the majority of the cases this is the whole time. In some cells this will mean that the children go into another room and perhaps watch a Christian video after a certain length of time, but they are always involved for a period.

Prayer ideas

Prayer times can be as creative as other times. As with most other things you will find that if the children's attention is held, so will the attention of many more of the adults be.

- Praying in twos or threes will mean everyone is involved.
- Everyone could be given five minutes to lead on a topic. Some children may need help to prepare this, as may some of the adults.
- Pray with action and drama, which can lead into prophetic prayer.
- Give children (and adults) the opportunity to understand properly what is being prayed about; use pictures, maps, letters, newspapers, photographs.
- Ask the children to help you prepare, do drawings, bring topics particularly relevant to them!
- Look back and see how God has answered prayer since the last time the group prayed. Children (and adults) love to hear stories and it builds faith. The Bible is full of stories about men of faith! How exciting to hear stories

of adults, young people and children in the cell who have seen the hand of God move through prayer!

- Include prayer about things that directly touch the lives of cell members.
- Put prayer topics in different parts of the house and let people move from one to the other – this could be rather like a treasure hunt, praying for four minutes at every place where the prayer treasure is found! (Adults enjoy this, too.)
- Go in twos or threes to different places in the vicinity and pray, for example outside different public buildings, shops, schools, around the hospital.
- Ask children (and adults) to write a letter to local people, such as the fire brigade, police, or councillors, asking what they would like prayer for. Pray over the replies – this could be an on-going project!

Twice a year we have a week of prayer. Each time the number of children attending builds up. They have the opportunity of sitting with their parents, or of sitting in a group with other children and a responsible adult who uses spontaneous creativity to help them focus.

I believe there will be a tremendous change in our nation when we come *together* on a regular basis to pray!

Fasting

Children can also be inspired and enjoy fasting! Our children and young people loved a forty-day fast for the whole church. Families agreed together to fast from many and varied things – television, computer games, secular music, puddings, sweets and so on. Some families spent extra time praying together, while others came to the church building to pray with members of their cell; some cells met for extra prayer too! It was a time of great rejoicing and breakthrough. It fills my heart with wonder that a generation will grow up with a good experience of prayer and fasting!

The intergenerational celebration

What about Sundays? There are no definitive answers to that question. Possibly what you decide to do will depend on the degree to which you have accepted the values that have been presented in this manual. Always start with the intergenerational cell, and once the children feel accepted there it is a good time to bring the cells together for celebrations. Some Churches will have intergenerational cells but take it no further. Every pastor must ask God for the way forward, but always it is essential to envision the whole Church so that they understand why a particular way is being taken.

However, as it is a question I am often asked, we can explore it briefly. At Ely Christian Fellowship we have committed to being an intergenerational

Church. That does not mean that we do everything together, but it is the basis from which we move. As the celebration is the coming together of the cells, and as our cells all carry the intergenerational value, we *all* come to the celebration to encounter the transcendent God. We don't want our children or young people to miss it. We need them to be there, they have their own unique contribution to make as the power of God is released among us.

As children (and adults) gain in confidence in the cell, as they find their gifts and are encouraged, so they will find that they are more confident in the celebration. All too often we have expected children to perform in the celebration rather than participate with adults. As there has been little place within the Church for this flow to be expressed between the generations it is hardly surprising that, as the whole body has come together, it has remained fragmented.

Without ownership and recognition children and young people have often seen the Sunday celebration as boring and irrelevant. They have wanted to be included, for it to be a lively expression of their vitality, and relevant to this time in their nation and in their lives and families. These values are not in opposition to what the Holy Spirit is wanting to do for all of us.

Description

Our celebration is one of powerful praise and worship. It is a time when we expect to see the power of God released and to hear the Word preached in a way that impacts us all. The children and youth are encouraged to take an active part and to present their vitality as their worship to God. When people hear of a celebration like this they often fear that it introduces childishness. We have not become childish in any way, but we do experience the release of childlike faith and spontaneous enthusiasm. Everyone may use banners, or streamers, and is free to express their worship to God.

Our worship team is made up of people of all ages. As the congregation looks at the stage they see an expression of all the generations. During the praise and worship other children may be given permission to join the worship team and sing with them for a short time. So the visual impact is that this is for *everyone*!

Jesus preached to all the generations, He did it by speaking the language of the people, by being visual, relevant and straight to the point. He said 'Look at the birds of the air . . . see how the lilies of the field grow'. He told stories, and spoke about the things He saw and the people He met on the way. Everyone was interested in what He said. This was 'intergenerational' preaching! In the celebration, where all ages are present, the only requirement is to preach like Jesus.

So preaching does not have to lose its power because it is aimed at all ages. Sometimes we involve the children and the youth, or have something visual or dramatic. Overhead projector slides can make an impact if they are informative and fun. It is important that the preacher chooses the words he uses carefully – no long words, no religious jargon that is difficult to under-stand – by adults and children alike! Incidentally the unchurched coming in will be more impacted too!

Sometimes the children are given a sheet to draw pictures about the preaching, or to have an 'I-spy' where there are things to look out for in the sermon (*examples of these can be found at the back of the book*). These are also much appreciated after the celebration is over. They can be taken to the cell meeting, given to the visiting speaker or sometimes the pastor takes a special interest in them. The best incentive to do them is that parents take notice of and value them!

Our children are not undisciplined, they are involved. Cells in turn are responsible for the ushering in the celebration, and so children, young people and adults are there to welcome those who come. They also help with things like serving communion.

At the back of our auditorium we have some soft chairs and toys (that do not make a noise!) This area is reserved for adults to take children under the age of 4 years, should they feel the need to do so. It is not secluded, or tucked in a corner, it is a part of the whole. I am sometimes asked, 'Shouldn't everything be "decently and in order"?' to which I reply that to keep a small child confined for that length of time is not 'decently and in order', it is child abuse! Very small children wander around, just as I expect they did with Jesus. They may find another adult they know, maybe a cell member, and sit on their lap a while before moving on. Just as in the cell meeting, the children belong to everyone.

When there is ministry, the children respond as they feel they should, or want to. Basically they have been shown that anything that is said 'from the front' applies to them also. They are often far more responsive than the adults! If someone is receiving prayer, then some children will go and pray for them too.

In the pre-celebration intercession they listen to what is asked of everyone . . . and do it.

May I encourage you by saying that our young people and children used to be bored and 'switched off' in the services, in fact many of them spent their time under the chairs with toys rather than participating. They had no owner-ship of the meeting and were sitting through a service that had adults as the sole focus. As we have started to consider the needs of younger generations so we see a benefit for adults who had also been 'switched off'.

The children have taken their place in the cell meeting and been accepted there, and as we have acknowledged them, so they have taken their place in the larger gathering.

At the front of the church there is always an adult who can help the children enter into worship creatively – the children dance, kneel, lie prostrate before God, or actively present their worship to God. They are encouraged by the adult responsible and the expectation is that every child will take an active part. The only bored children are those who are spectators, not partakers (as with adults!) Some children choose to sit at the front while others remain with their parents, or another responsible adult.

This adult is not responsible for leading the children, but rather for facilitating their flowing with the leadership of the celebration. They will encourage them to respond to anything said at the front, to respond creatively to the songs that are being sung, to check out any contribution they may feel that they have for the body, for example, prophecy.

Timetable

The following is what we currently do on Sundays, though we are always open to change:

10 am	Youth cells meet in homes (though we anticipate these moving to a Saturday evening).
10-10.15 am	Intercession for adults and children.
10.15-10.50 am	Children's cells/groups, led by children, meet in the church building, or family interactive session called 'Word Alive!' Adults have Bible teaching.
10.50-11.15 am	Coffee break.
11.15am	Celebration for everyone, including the youth, who have returned to the building.

This description is at the time of going to press; we are conscious of moving on all the time in ways that the Lord shows us to 'bind us together with cords that cannot be broken'.

Worship leading

Listed below are some considerations for worship leaders of intergenerational celebrations.

- You are there to lead *everyone* to the throne of God, and, as shepherd of the flock, it will be essential for you to see where the sheep are. Worship leaders who lead with their eyes closed are largely oblivious to the sheep! Similarly it is difficult to follow someone who can't be seen or who moves so quickly that it is impossible to keep up with them. So it is important that the worship leader has a real understanding of why the whole family of God has gathered together and expresses pleasure in that.

- As previously stated this is not a time specifically for children's songs. Our children love current prophetic songs, worship and praise. However, to have many songs with numerous verses can lead to the children (and some adults) getting lost in the words. To include one or two songs of that sort is acceptable if they are interspersed with others that are easily repeated. Starting with a song that everyone knows is good as it gives 'lift off' to everyone!

- Many churches sing one song repeatedly and this can be a good thing; however, when children are present, and the same could apply to many adults, it is important to keep variety, so flowing on from one song to another after a few repetitions will help the children to stay focused (and some adults too).

- Another essential is to have someone pointing to the words if an overhead projector or something similar is used. This will help all children to read the words and find the place again if the song has repetitions.

- Who is in the worship team? Do you have a mixture of people of different ages? Worship is more than singing and there may be many who are worshippers but do not have voices that would be acceptable to the usual standards of a worship team. Currently we have different groups who sing with the 'official' worship team but only have one microphone between them. This enables anyone, of any age, to sing on the stage and lead the congregation. They attend the worship practice on a Monday night to praise, pray and worship God together – children, young people and adults. This makes a powerful statement that the celebration is for everyone.

- Above all, pray that God will unite the 'whole nation of God' as your Church comes together, and have faith and vision for this unity to be corporately expressed.

Chapter 6

Would You Tell _____ Me About . . . ? _____

There are some questions that come up in relation to establishing intergenerational cells wherever I go, and below I have answered some of the most common ones.

Sponsoring in the intergenerational cell

In the Cell Church, equipping and training people on a one-to-one basis is foundational to the personal and corporate growth of the cell. While children are still forming their value systems, adults and young people are already entrenched in theirs.

Sponsoring is when two people enter into a relationship, or friendship, and within that context one takes the other through, or they share together, books that will challenge their values, and introduce them to cell life. These pairs will be adult to adult, young person to young person/adult, and child to adult or responsible young person.

Books to explain this further are available (*An equipping track for adults*, and *'Passion' for youth*, see Bibliography). *Living with Jesus* takes children on that journey, these booklets helping them to examine their values, identify their strongholds and introduce them to the Cell Church, as they meet regularly with an older responsible person. The Sponsor's, or Befriender's, Guide explains this in more detail.

The number of children in a cell

There is no prescribed number of children for any cell, but perhaps the easiest way to decide how many a cell should have is to think 'family'. Each family, generally(!), decides how many children to have, how many they can happily love and care for. So it is with cell. Some will decide that they are very happy with many children, while others will decide that they can only cope with a few. This factor will need to be taken into consideration by each cell when deciding when to multiply. For this purpose teenagers are considered as adults.

Ownership

Every member needs to feel that the cell belongs to them, and, as in a family, they are able to 'do their bit'. What can the cell members, adults, young people and children, share? Each cell has a list of tasks, or ministries, that can be shared out on a rota (see form in Appendix 3). Children can take ownership of most, but not all, activities on the list, but that is equally true of some adults.

Ownership is also about developing in ministry, and being responsible for the ministry in the cell.

It is advisable for each person to have their assigned ministry, for that is what the tasks are, for a set period of time – six to eight weeks is a good period, as that gives everyone time to fail and then succeed, or to develop their ministry in their own special way. This results in each member

- being able to improve and experiment.
- being able to develop creatively.
- being able to fail and then to learn from their mistakes.
- gaining in confidence in an area and being able to pass on their experience to the next person, i.e. training another person.

How do you know what children can cope with? The same way that you find out what an adult can manage – by giving them responsibility. Most adults and children do not know what they can do until they try!

Another area of ownership is in the corporate life of the Church. Some examples of this are:

- When a cell has a member who is getting married, it is the cell's wedding and everyone becomes involved – even in the clearing up!
- In the celebration each cell in turn may do the ushering – children make excellent ushers.
- When the Lord's Supper is celebrated, children, adults and young people can be part of serving in whatever way is appropriate for your church.

It is so much fun when the cell works together and Church becomes theirs.

Baptism

I will not attempt to go into great detail about this here. My book, *When a child asks to be baptised*, addresses baptism and the part that cell can play. However, suffice it to say that it is 'as with adults'!

The time of the meeting

Every family will have different ideas about appropriate bedtimes for children; every person will have different problems to work through such as men who commute, elderly who do not like going out after dark, young people with homework. It is not possible to decree an optimum time; every cell must find its own best time. There are always ways to accommodate the differing needs of members. The following are just some ideas:

- Sunday or Saturday teatime or early evening.
- A weekday with the men coming straight from work, perhaps with a snack.
- Everyone eating together before the meeting.
- Perhaps 7 pm to 9 pm, agreeing that one late night a week is acceptable.

I have never found a cell that has not been able to accommodate everyone if they really believe in the value of the cell all meeting together.

Children who do not want to attend

As with adults! Encourage them with friendship, spend time with them in the week, love them, pray for them, find out if there is a problem. Go straight to them rather than sending messages via their parents, as this will confirm to them that they are important. If everything is filtered through the parents children will receive the message that people are not directly interested in them. In our experience, once they get involved in the life of the cell, they love it. (As with the adults!)

Adults who want to share problems

In my experience children know about most of the problems that are around, but do not get an opportunity to be part of ministry, or to see the prayer that will bring the answer. In 2 Chronicles 20:13 God called *everyone* to face the crises. If children grow up seeing the hand of God in problems and seeing Him work miracles, they are going to be better equipped to face their own problems in the future.

However, if a problem is unsuitable for sharing in front of the children, it is probably unsuitable for sharing in the cell meeting, and should be left to another occasion. Having children present helps to create good boundaries with cell members who would want to divulge everything to everyone all the time!

Small children and babies

Children need to experience being part of the cell meeting from birth. Imagine a generation growing up among people who love and accept them, worshipping God and knowing His presence.

Little ones love to be part of the icebreaker and worship, and then go off to sleep in a different room, or even on their parents' laps, or at their feet! This introduces them to the cell meeting and allows the parents to see when they are ready to be present for longer.

Very small babies can be taken to the meeting in their prams or travel cots.

If the meeting is held earlier in the day, for instance at Sunday teatime, then another answer would be to have a Kids' Slot (see page 60). This would allow the little ones to be taken out during the Word and Witness sections of the meeting. In this situation every member should take a turn at caring for them. Cell is about the love of Jesus in our relationships. These little ones need relationship with all the cell members and all the cell members need relationship with the little ones.

Disruptive children or families who find it hard to cope

Remember that cell is about more than a meeting. Just as an unbeliever would not attend the meeting until they were ready, the same principle could apply in this instance. A child might attend for just a short time, as with very small children; families can be included in the lives of cell members, for example by inviting the mother for coffee, or the father to go fishing, the child on an outing.

If they are Christians, the first priority is to ensure that they are being sponsored, each member of the family building a relationship with another person in the cell and deepening their relationship with God and man as they work through sponsoring materials.

Look for God-given strategies.

Introducing children to functioning cells

The first question to ask is 'Has the whole cell looked at the values and Scriptural foundation for the generations coming together?' Once the cell has prayed these through, shared together, and understood that this is spiritual warfare, then it is a good time to introduce them to some of the principles that are foundational to cell and into which the children will need to be accepted. These principles are outlined in this book but some of the most important are

- that Cell Church is a move of God, and introducing the children is as much for the benefit of adults as for the children.
- the 'as with adults' principle.
- available options, like the Kids' Slot, which could be introduced for all the children with the option of keeping children in with the adults and young people as they become ready.

Chapter 7

_____ And Finally! _____

When people ask me if I am sure that this will work, I never hesitate to answer that it *must*. I see no other answer in Scripture than that we come together, I see no better way for our children to learn and be included, and I see the Spirit of God bringing an awareness of this to the body of Christ that has hitherto been lacking.

Ely is not the only place where this vision is being pursued. As I travel I see more and more churches prayerfully starting to take this route. I would like to end firstly by quoting from reports written by visitors to our church; not because we have 'got it all together', for we will always be seeking the face of God to show us how and where we can prepare more adequately to be the pure and spotless bride for the Son of God, but because Ely is my home and the place that I am privileged to be part of. It is always interesting to see what other people say about us, for sometimes we do not 'see the wood for the trees' and their observations, I hope, will bring life to what has been expressed in this book. The comments are grouped under the activity to which they refer, and are quoted verbatim.

Intercession
'Before the meeting there was a time for the church to pray. This was by no means attended by everyone (which was encouraging) but there were a number of children and young people there along with adults. Prayer was active and exuberant, for instance we spent some time walking around the building, praying over some of the seats for the people who would occupy them that morning.'

'Sunday morning began at 10 am with everyone together (adults and children) for 15 minutes of intercession. The children were encouraged to pray just as the adults, i.e. aloud or quietly, in tongues or English, standing or walking.

'Significantly, they were encouraged, both at this time and at the later celebration, to gather around a key adult at the front of the church, or be with a parent or responsible adult, and not be either uninvolved or just allowed to run around. The church rightly sees discipline as important.

'Another key feature of this church is that most children, most of the time, are both involved and well behaved. I did not come across the "this is boring" syndrome that many children exhibit even in so-called "lively" churches. They were well behaved because they were interested and involved, and they were interested and involved because they were valued as equal participants and included on every possible occasion.'

The celebration

'A time of praise and worship, followed by a message for everyone. The children either sat at the front or with their parents. Those at the front were actively encouraged to participate, for example by joining in the prayers with loud amens, picking up on specific songs and emphasising them verbally or dramatically, kneeling in worship, lying prostrate, waving flags, dancing, marching, etc. During the preaching everyone from the very youngest to the oldest is encouraged to take notes, or draw pictures to remind them of what is being preached. This enables everyone to participate in the "life application" section of the cell meeting during the following week. The message is presented in as interactive a way as possible – for example specific points were dramatised or illustrated, people were bought to the front and used as a demonstration.'

'The celebration meeting was a good quality, modern, charismatic meeting, full of spiritual life and vitality, and therefore I would want to restrict my comments to the intergenerational Cell Church aspects of it.

'Despite being 200-plus people present, there was an atmosphere of warmth and oneness that reflected, I believe, the strength of the bottom-up model of cell church organisation, consisting of cells that themselves are church, building quality relationships, now coming together to worship. I noted in particular that we were welcomed into church by one of the church's intergenerational cells, both children and adults, who were responsible for welcoming that week . . . there was no slow warm-up of people worship-ping – they went straight in. All children above toddler age were encouraged to worship – and most did, as did the youth! There were no children's songs, but there is a church policy of choosing songs that include ones that children could more easily pick up or participate in by waving, dancing, shouting, using banners, etc. One simple but interesting point that I noticed during the worship was that the person operating the overhead projector pointed to the words along the line, as a teacher of primary school children would, to help them read the words. This shows the care that the church takes in pursuing its philosophy of including the children. It is also important to note that this celebration was not a family service geared to children, but an inclusive celebration for all age groups and what the adults did the children were encouraged to do and vice versa.

'The word . . . was preached at an adult level in the sense that there was no talking down to the children, but the language was simple and direct which, I am sure, was helpful to both adults and children. Examples . . . were drawn from children's, youth and adult experiences. The children and youth were fully involved in this message and a most impressive feature was that almost all above toddler stage made notes on the sermon in readiness for following the subject through in cell group later in the week. The message lasted for 40/45 minutes . . . the word held the children's, youth and adult interest throughout and had a good life application thrust to it.'

The cell prayer meetings

'These are half-hour meetings of the cell for prayer which are held weekly in addition to the cell meeting, at a convenient time for cell members. All cell members are normally expected to attend.

'I attended two of these prayer meetings. Both prayer meetings were inspiring meetings to attend and yet were very different. On Sunday we broke down into groups of four people to pray for each other's needs, and then into twos to pray for each other's unchurched contacts. I prayed with a thirteen-year-old girl who was not embarrassed by my age or church leadership position, and who initiated the praying by praying in the Spirit, and then for my contacts. I was impressed by her maturity and genuineness.

'The Monday group's praying centred mainly on issues raised by the group as a whole and in particular prayer for the very sick family member of one member of the group. Prayer took on a 'warfare mode' and virtually every member, including the children and youth, contributed aloud. Again spiritual gifts were manifest freely. I was again impressed by the confidence and authority of the children's and youth contributions.'

The cell meeting

'We were welcomed effectively by the children . . . we worshipped and God was with us, the children were responsible for the offering.

'The Word began as open contributions from all members of the group . . . I was amazed at the group's ability, with the aid of their notes from Sunday, to contribute to the meeting. I can say with the authority of thirty-three years' experience in primary and secondary school that these children and young people were not just regurgitating facts, but were making valid contributions to the meeting, including referring back to the Sunday's Bible verses.

'The group then broke down into small groups to pray for those in the group . . . and showed particular love and care for one member who was quite "down".

'Here is a church that is seriously committed to cell philosophy and values and to working those through in an intergenerational environment, and is succeeding.' *Glory to God!*

'I spent a full weekend with the church and the leaders at Ely to see how it worked at ground level. I spent a full weekend with the church and leaders – listening, watching and learning. I thoroughly enjoyed the whole time, but the real highlight for me was when I experienced an all-age cell group meeting. As a visitor I felt instantly welcomed and part of what went on. The children and youth were as much a part of it as anyone else. When the group prayed for me the children gathered around me and laid hands on me. The presence of Jesus was so tangible and it moved me to tears as my young brothers and sisters in Christ ministered to me – I will never forget the experience.

'What grips me are the thoroughly biblical values and principles which are foundational to the working out of intergenerational cells. If the body of Christ gets hold of these values we will see a power Church emerge as a testimony in an age where relationships break down and the generations are separated. What I got a glimpse of in Ely fellowship excites me – the principles do work!'

Conclusion

Whilst all these reports are encouraging, we know that we do not have all the answers and we walk humbly before God in what He has given us – but we are here to help in any way we can. We do not promise that it will be easy, but we can promise that, if you pray and hold closely to the God-given vision, it will be possible for the body of Christ where you are to be united and for the 'hearts of the fathers to be turned to the children and the hearts of the children to the fathers.' (Malachi 4)

> How good and pleasant it is when brothers live together in unity! It is like precious oil . . . it is as if the dew of Hermon were falling on Mount Zion. For there the Lord bestows his blessing, even life for evermore. (Psalm 133)

> My prayer is . . . that all of them may be one, Father, just as you are in me and I am in you. May they also be in us so that the world may believe that you have sent me. I have given them the glory that you gave me, that they may be one as we are one: I in them and you in me. May they be brought to complete unity to let the world know that you sent me and have loved them even as you have loved me. (John 17:20-23)

Bibliography and
___ Recommended Reading ___

The second reformation, William A. Beckham, published by TOUCH Publications, PO Box 19888, Houston TX77224.

Where do we go from here? Ralph W. Neighbour, published by TOUCH Publications.

The shepherd's guidebook, Ralph W. Neighbour, published by TOUCH Publications.

Sowing, reaping, keeping, by Laurence Singlehurst, published by Crossway Books, an imprint of IVP, Norton Street, Nottingham NG7 3HR.

Cell iT, by Laurence Singlehurst, *An equipping track for adults, 'Passion' for youth,* and *CellChurch Magazine* are all available from the Lighthouse Centre, 13 Lynn Road, Ely, Cambridgeshire CB7 4EG.

Materials for facilitating cell meetings and for helping to include the children are available from Daphne Kirk at The Lighthouse Centre, 13 Lynn Road, Ely, Cambridgeshire CB7 4EG. See Appendix 2 for further details.

Appendix 1

_____ Seminars _____

These seminars are for you if you can identify with any of the following:

- Have you wondered how to integrate your children and young people totally into the body of Christ?
- Are you lacking the resources and training and therefore unsure of the way forward?
- Do you wonder how your church can have one vision and move together, adults, young people and children?
- Do you want your whole church to grow, learn and experience kingdom life in the way God intended . . . together?
- Are you cell church and wanting to integrate the children?

Important points with regard to seminars:

(a) The seminars are visionary with a strong biblical foundation as well as very practical, with their emphasis being on the outworking of the vision in the local church.

(b) It is essential for the senior leadership to attend the seminar in order to carry the vision to their own congregation. However, the format is kept simple so that anyone can participate and lead intergenerational groups.

(c) Seminars vary between one and three days, depending on the number of workshops held. Obviously the longer the seminar, the more practical experience and personal application can be incorporated. Churches usually have seminars for Friday evening and all day Saturday.

(d) Seminars include discussion of, and where possible some experience of, the intergenerational celebration and corporate prayer life of the church. Leaders of worship, celebration and prayer meetings are strongly encouraged to attend.

(e) A manual will be used so that leaders can replicate the seminar with their own church. However, the more people from your church who attend the seminar, the clearer will be the vision and the greater the anointing taken back.

If you are considering being an intergenerational church or having intergenerational cells and would like to host or attend one of Daphne Kirk's seminars contact her at:

The Lighthouse Centre
13 Lynn Road
Ely
Cambs
CB7 4EG

Telephone: 01353 662228
Fax: 01353 662179
E-mail: ecf@lhouse.win-uk.net

Appendix 2

Materials Available to Facilitate the Intergenerational Cell

There are currently two books of meeting outlines:

Book 1

- Relationships (based on the Book of Ruth)
- Extracts from 1 Timothy

Book 2

- Who will be a servant?
- The Lord's Supper
- Prayer

Each pack consists of meeting outlines, each section being a series for four weeks. These give detailed instructions on every section of the meeting, including the icebreaker and the offering.

Living with Jesus: sponsoring/discipling children through their own equipping track.

Befriending a child: a guide to sponsoring/discipling children through their own equipping track.

When a child asks to be baptised: Is the child ready? What about the parents? What place can the cell have? How can we help the child understand?

Available from:

The Lighthouse Centre, 13 Lynn Road, Ely, Cambs CB7 4EG

Telephone: 01353 662228
Fax: 01353 662179
E-mail: ecf@lhouse.win-uk.net

Appendix 3

Forms . . .

. . . for ideas,

to photocopy,

or just to browse through!

Cell Meeting for _____ (date)

To be prayed over by you and the leadership team.

Cell Leaders _____   Cell Leaders _____
                                                                    (*in training*)

_____   _____

Meeting started at _____ and ended at _____

Members absent	Reason for absence

New attenders	Notes

General report of the meeting
(Overall spirit, most significant events, weaknesses or problems)

Interaction during the week (past and present)

Pastoral, members (is it inclusive or cliquish), etc

Sponsoring and accountability

Please list people being sponsored and who by. Then give a brief report on progress.

Please list accountability partners and give brief report on progress

If you have most of your group involved, please list them a few each week

Youth

E.g. Are they participating, problems, encouragements, etc

Have you asked about and prayed for their Youth Cells?

Children *Name of person responsible this series* _____
(Are they participating/any problems/are they having interaction with members between meetings?)

Have you asked about, and prayed for your Children's cell meeting?

Prayer meetings *Name of person responsible this series* _____

Dates _____   Venues _____
_____   _____
Total Number: adults _____   secondary school _____
primary school _____

Worship *Name of person responsible for this series* _____

Ministry *Name of person responsible for this series* _____

Word (Life application)

Please state if anyone other than the Cell Leader took this _____

Any comments on this series in particular?

Witness (Works) and evangelism in the group generally

Names of people responsible for this series _____
Please be specific about plans for and reports on group evangelism, social outreach events and personal evangelism, etc

How are you?

Is there anything you would particularly like help for? Are you OK? Any personal encouragements, etc?

Cell Meeting Attendance Record

(It is recommended that this be filled in by the Co-ordinator
using the Meeting Evaluation Form)

Series commencing _____ and ending _____

Please list married couples and all children individually

Weeks

Name	1	2	3	4	5	6

Member's Information

Name _____ Date of birth _____

Address _____

_____

_____

Tel no: _____

Marital status _____

Occupation _____ Work tel no: _____

Driver Yes/No _____ Car owner Yes/No _____

Children	D.O.B.	School	Cell

Cell Leader _____ Date _____

Cell Leader _____ Date _____

Cell Leader _____ Date _____

Member's Information
(Youth/Children)

Name _____ Date of birth _____

Address _____

_____

_____

Tel no: _____

School/College _____

Do parents attend a cell (please specify) _____

Are parents/carers Born Again _____

Parents'/Carers' name _____

Relationships _____

Brothers/Sisters (name and age) _____

_____

Do they attend a cell? _____

Cell Leader _____ Date _____

Cell Leader _____ Date _____

Cell Leader _____ Date _____

Cell Leader _____ Date _____

Hosting Schedule

Cell Leaders _____

Co-ordinator _____

Meeting Night this series _____

Person responsible for Hosting Schedule _____

Number of copies required from the office _____

Date	Name	Address	Phone No.

Cell Responsibilities for this series

The Cell Leader remains responsible for Word (personal aplication),
Evaluation forms, Pastoral strategy, Sponsoring/Accountability

Hosting Schedule (put in file for copying) _____

Prayer Chain (put in file for copying) _____

Cell Prayer Meetings (arrange weekly) _____

Birthdays (see Cell Leader) _____

Transport (arrange as necessary) _____

Ushering (remind Cell and head up) _____

Notices (collect from Cell Leader) _____

Icebreaker _____

Worship (15 minutes, be creative) _____

Offering (bring an attractive container) _____

Ministry (15 minutes) _____

Witness (15 minutes) _____

Children's Co-ordinator
(check children included and OK) _____

Social Interaction (check all included,
arrange social event) _____

Evangelism (individual and group outreach) _____

Anything else! _____

Any member unable to fulfil their
responsibility any particular week should
find a substitute themselves and notify _____

Prayer and Communication Chain

Cell Leader(s) _____

Names should be entered as families, families pray together!

(Please phone the person whose name appears after yours on the prayer chain.)

Name _____ Phone No. _____

Name _____ Phone No. _____

Name _____ Phone No. _____

Name _____ Phone No. _____

Name _____ Phone No. _____

Name _____ Phone No. _____

Name _____ Phone No. _____

Name _____ Phone No. _____

Name _____ Phone No. _____

Name _____ Phone No. _____

Name _____ Phone No. _____

last person phones the person at the top of the list!

If you are unable to contact the person under your name, ring the next available person, and keep trying to contact the person who was unavailable!

Youth Cells

Feedback for prayer by you and other leaders.

Leaders' names _____

Venue _____ Date _____

Who Attended

Absences and response you will make to their absence . . .

How did the meeting go?

Name two high points

Name two low points

Anything you need help with?

Planned social get-together . . .

How are both of you?

Youth Cells Hosting Schedule

Youth Cell Leaders _____

Co-ordinator _____

Meeting Night this series _____

Person responsible for Hosting Schedule _____

Number of copies required from the office _____

Date	Name	Address	Phone No.

Youth Cell Meeting Attendance Record

(It is recommended that this be filled in by the Co-ordinator
using the Meeting Evaluation Form)

Series commencing _____ and ending _____

Weeks

Name	1	2	3	4	5	6

Youth Cells Responsibilities for the series

_____ to _____

Cell leader remains responsible for Cell Meeting, Evaluation forms,
Pastoral Strategy, Sponsoring/Accountability

Hosting Schedule (put in file for copying) _____

Prayer Chain (put in file for copying)   _____

Prayer Meetings   _____

Birthdays   _____

Transport   _____

Notices (collect from Cell Leader)   _____

Icebreaker   _____

Worship   _____

Social Interaction (check everyone
included, arrange social events)   _____

Evangelism and group outreach   _____

Anything else!   _____

Anyone unable to fulfil their responsibility
any particular week should find a
substitute themselves and notify   _____

Prayer and Communication Chain

Youth Cell Leader(s) _____

(Please phone the person whose name appears after yours on the prayer chain.)

Name _____ Phone No. _____

Name _____ Phone No. _____

Name _____ Phone No. _____

Name _____ Phone No. _____

Name _____ Phone No. _____

Name _____ Phone No. _____

Name _____ Phone No. _____

Name _____ Phone No. _____

Name _____ Phone No. _____

Name _____ Phone No. _____

Name _____ Phone No. _____

last person phones the person at the top of the list!

If you are unable to contact the person under your name, ring the next available person, and keep trying to contact the person who was unavailable!

Word (personal application)

Notes for Cell Leader

Week commencing Sunday _____

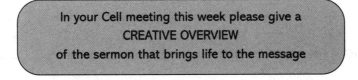

> In your Cell meeting this week please give a
> **CREATIVE OVERVIEW**
> of the sermon that brings life to the message

Always refer to your notes that you took on Sunday, as this models their value. Always look at the children's notes or pictures and put them in the special file.
Tell them that the Pastors would love to see the file at the end of the series (they will put stickers on and comment on them before returning them to the group). NB: If adults and youth want to include theirs in the file that would be wonderful too!

Remember that most of the members have already heard the sermon and do not need a repeat!

Those who were not present on Sunday are needing to hear the main Scriptures and how people were challenged, or changed, as that is the basis of the Cell meeting.

Creative ideas

- Ask each person to share one thing from their 'sermon notes'.
- Have a short quiz (make sure that the questions are going to promote application, not study!)
- Prepare a short sketch to illustrate the main theme.
- Bring a visual aid either similar to the one used by the preacher, or bring your own.
- Ask the children to show their sheets and talk about what they have on them.
- Pass a sheet of paper round and ask each person to write one thing that really impacted them, turn it over, and pass it to the next person . . . then read it to the group (like a game of 'consequences').
- Give an incomplete sentence and ask each member to complete it. E.g. 'After the sermon on Sunday I never again want to . . .'
  'The thing I heard that has made a difference to me is . . .'
- Write four of the main words on a piece of paper and ask two or three people to talk for 30 seconds on what one of those words meant to them.

This form is completed by the person preaching and given
to all Cell Leaders after the Sunday Celebration

Cell Meeting

Sermon on Sunday _____

Main Scriptures _____

_____

Theme _____

Questions for the Cell Meeting

_____

_____

_____

_____

Children: Take this sheet to your Life Group this week so you can talk about some of the things said in the sermon this week that were really important to you. You may use writing or drawings, whichever you like!

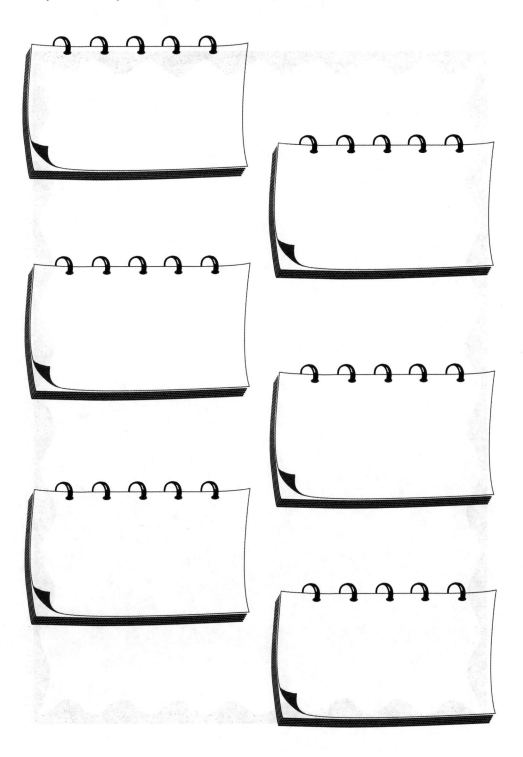

Adults: For the next few weeks the Life Application in your Life Groups will be sharing about how the sermon impacted you. If you would like to make some notes this may help you to share more fully!

Youth: In the next few weeks we will be sharing in our Life Groups about how the sermon could change us in some way. This sheet is for you to make notes or do a sketch, about something you heard so that you will have a reminder on your meeting night.